T0208700

COACHING IS SERVANT LEADERSHIP

Dr. Anita S. Greenlee

WESTBOW
PRESS®
A DIVISION OF THOMAS NELSON
& ZONDERVAN

Scripture quotations are from the ESV® Bible (The Holy Bible, English Standard Version®), copyright © 2001 by Crossway, a publishing ministry of Good News Publishers. Used by permission. All rights reserved.

This book is a work of non-fiction. Unless otherwise noted, the author and the publisher make no explicit guarantees as to the accuracy of the information contained in this book and in some cases, names of people and places have been altered to protect their privacy.

WestBow Press books may be ordered through booksellers or by contacting:

WestBow Press
A Division of Thomas Nelson & Zondervan
1663 Liberty Drive
Bloomington, IN 47403
www.westbowpress.com
1 (866) 928-1240

Because of the dynamic nature of the Internet, any web addresses or links contained in this book may have changed since publication and may no longer be valid. The views expressed in this work are solely those of the author and do not necessarily reflect the views of the publisher, and the publisher hereby disclaims any responsibility for them.

Any people depicted in stock imagery provided by Getty Images are models, and such images are being used for illustrative purposes only. Certain stock imagery © Getty Images.

ISBN: 978-1-9736-4963-2 (sc)
ISBN: 978-1-9736-4964-9 (hc)
ISBN: 978-1-9736-4962-5 (e)

Library of Congress Control Number: 2018914944

Print information available on the last page.

WestBow Press rev. date: 01/15/2019

I dedicate this work to God, who is faithful, who provided me with strength I did not know was in me, and who displayed a gentle touch by wiping away my tears, reminding me fear does not reside in believers. He is my El Elyon for healing my body and keeping me on the course and time prescribed before I was born.

I dedicate this to my best friend, my confidant, my loudest encourager and cheerleader, one who is most gentle and full of wisdom, loving, caring, but most of all, the one who constantly prays for me and encourages me when life moves fast. My husband, Mark, you are indeed the wind beneath my wings and my rock on earth. God knew the special assignment he placed in you for me. Mark, your love, patience, sacrifices, and bravery to do life with me takes my breath away.

I dedicate this to my big guy—Mark John II. You are indeed a blessing. Big guy, thanks for being a gentle and praying son who encourages me with your smiles and kisses every day. Thanks for understanding when Mom needed time to read and write and for waiting to have supper on our date because you wanted me to take a break and enjoy you.

I dedicate this to my first mentor, teacher, and coach and the person who lived a life as a servant to and for many, my mother "Norma," whom I miss dearly. Thank you for always reminding me when I was weary, "You are doing fine, Suga; just relax!" I dedicate this to my father "James"; being a daddy's girl made me who I am today. I miss you.

I dedicate this is to my brothers and sister who understood why I could not make every family gathering and still loved me.

I dedicate this to Nicole Brown, for showing me what it means to work toward success and for keeping me looking good. I dedicate this to an impressive council of intercessors, my accountability group and prayer warriors—Pastor Yvonne "Mother" Daniel, former Pastors Kenneth and Cynthia Barbour, Minister Beverly Johnson (my best friend), Pastor Mary McGee, Minister Valarie Turner, Minister Maria Bradley, Mike and Pastor Alicia Evans, and Elder Christopher and Evangelist Bridgette White. To Pastors Tony and Cynthia Brazelton for your prayer. To Elders Mike and Georgia Bouie, thank you for encouraging me, praying for me, listening, keeping me fit, loving me just the way I am, and keeping the sun out of my eyes. Melanie Bedogne, thank you for honesty, bravery, and prayers while editing my freshman book.

I dedicate this to my professor and patient chair, Dr. Diane Wiater. In my mind, you were also my coach. Thank for you challenging me for the last two years in class and being a thinking partner who did not judge me or allow me to stop short. Thank you for making me reach into areas that are not my comfort zone while encouraging me to find the voice given to me for what God has called me to do. Dr. Wiater, thanks for believing in me and for taking every one of my calls, which calmed my inner storms. I also dedicate my freshman work to Dr. Kathleen Patterson, the one who sparked the fire of explaining what servant leadership is, which allowed me to thirst more for Jesus's way as a coach.

CONTENTS

CHAPTER 1
What Is Coaching, and Why Is It Important?

I can do all things through him who strengthens me.
—Philippians 4:13 (ESV)

Iron sharpens iron, and one man sharpens another.
—Proverbs 27:17 (ESV)

The coaching profession is experiencing explosive growth in the United States and abroad. Professional coaching centers have the goal of unlocking an individual's potential to maximize his or her performance.

Paul's teaching to the Philippians spoke of such a life. He encouraged all believers by saying that real joy does not come from man but from God, who gives inspiration and desires that believers do all things according to His will. The message Paul delivered was one of hope in Philippians 4:13; this verse speaks of living a full life that is powered by faith. Paul also encouraged his readers by saying that sufficiency is given when you believe. In Proverbs 27:15, Solomon teaches the importance of engaging individuals ("Iron sharpens iron") who are willing to assist others in reaching their full potential.

Solomon's message is still relevant; there is still a need for wise counsel. Such individuals will ask thought-provoking questions that cause them to look in a realistic manner at where they currently are in relation to where they desire to be. This level of reflection requires a relationship with a thinking partner who is willing to allow you to think out loud without judgment or to allow your position, whether great or small, to interfere with your desires.

Coaching has an extensive history that traces back to the Bible. In the Bible, we see examples of coaching in the way God interacted with Adam, with Jesus, and then with the twelve disciples. In the 1960s, modern-day coaching was known as developmental counseling; since then, it has evolved into developmental coaching. The primary foci of coaching improve and develop skills for the purpose of making better decisions. In recent years, coaching has become explosive due to its ability to bring about change that is both needed and accepted. Leadership coaching is an acceptable way to achieve a particular strategy, improve performances, and simply assist individuals in their personal lives to reach another level. Coaching does not tell others to come prepared to provide answers. Coaching leads the "coachee" to think of other ways to reach his or her goals. Coaching prompts thought-provoking questions to assist in moving the coachee forward. Linda Miller and Chad Hall, the authors of 2007's *Coaching for Christian Leaders: A Practical Guide*, believe a coach is an individual who assists actions that move people from one place to another, from where they are to a new purpose. It is essential for leaders to understand the definition of coaching, the origin of coaching, what coaching is and is not, why coaching is essential, and skills needed in coaching. Coaching develops, improves performances and behaviors, and causes an awareness that facilitates greater decision-making skills through goal setting and designing action plans.

Coaching is initiated when either an individual or an organization recognizes the need to improve. The search for a coach often starts with questions, such as the following:

1. What kind of coach is needed to assist with ongoing personnel, team, or organizational issues?
2. Is the coach going to assist with leadership or performance?
3. What do leadership development and coaching entail?

4. What should a potential client or coachee look for in a coach?
5. Does it matter if the coach is internal or external?
6. What should I expect from a coach?
7. Are there particular skills, certifications, and education that professional coaches are supposed to have?

Coach, coaching, mentor, mentoring, teaching, assessments, discipleship, servant, and *servant leadership* are terms that will be used throughout this book to discuss the topic of coaching. Before we go farther, let me explain what coaching is and why is it essential in faith-based/religious organizations.

▍DEFINITION OF COACHING

Coaching has been defined in varying ways by various people. In my quest to define coaching and the significance of its impact, I found it interesting to learn why many have various interpretations of the word. In the 2011 book *Handbook of Coaching Psychology: A Guide for Practitioners,* authors Stephen Palmer and Alison Whybrow differentiate coaching from coaching psychology. They define coaching as a means of unlocking potential to maximize an individual's performance; it is an action in facilitating performance, learning, and development within an individual. Coaching is defined as concern with the immediate improvement of both performance and development of skills. While there are myriad definitions of coaching, Sharon Ting and Peter Scisco, the editors of *The CCL Handbook for Coaching: A Guide for the Leader Coach* (2006), begin by describing coaching as an engaging relationship between individuals who aspire to improve or become more impactful in their leadership. These authors agree with the fundamental aspects of leadership coaching, which develops and empowers adult learners, helping them gain clarity about themselves and assisting them to make better decisions. Ting and Scisco provide explanations for the effectiveness of coaching in leadership development, describe the technical components of the coaching relationship, explain how populations benefit from coaching, and offer approaches that are traditional and tailored for the organization.

Tony Stoltzfus, the author of *Leadership Coaching: The Disciplines, Skills, and Heart of a Christian Coach* (2005), defines coaching from a faith-based perspective: Coaching develops and provides clarity to individuals for how their purpose fits with the broader mission of God. Stoltzfus further explains the coaching paradigm and the coaching process and reveals what God is doing with coaching globally. Dr. Gary Collins, Christian coach, speaker, and author of *Christian Coaching: Helping Others Turn Potential into Reality* (2002), defines Christian coaching as a practice that guides and enables individuals or groups to move from where they are to where God plans for them. Collins further suggests Christian coaches listen intently for messages that might come from God in researching the scriptures to discern what is right.

THE ORIGIN OF COACHING

Dr. Vicki Brock, the author of *Professional Challenges Facing the Coaching Field from a Historical Perspective* (2016), believes coaching as a modern profession emerged in the late twentieth century because of changes in the socioeconomic environment, nourished by the root disciplines of psychology, business, sports, and adult education. Coaching has rapidly entered the global mainstream during the twenty-first century, surrounded by an increase of training organizations, professional associates, and the material of evidence-based coaching. Coaching initially made its debut in the 1960s. Coaching emerged in business in the late 1970s because of changes in leadership models and organizational culture. Catapult to years later to when coaching took root outside of companies in the form of human potential and self-help. Coaching nestles academics, values, principles, and philosophical prescriptions from nonacademic areas. Brock further suggests earlier coaching was once labeled as counseling, an act that happened behind closed doors.

WHAT IS COACHING?

The late Sir John Whitmore, the author of 2009's *Coaching for Performance: GROWing Human Potential and Purpose*, believed coaching unlocks an individual's potential to maximize performance. With such a perspective, I challenge my readers to shift from thinking of coaching merely as a developmental tool used in business settings to be an effective method of personal development that can be used in faith-based organizations. Coaching develops! Coaching is moving individuals from where they currently are to where they ought to be!

As a leader who has served in many positions in the church, business, and military, I know and have experienced personally that coaching is a useful tool. I am an advocate for developing skills, exploring possibilities, enhancing capacity, and tapping into the maximum potential of individuals, especially those serving in leadership positions. Most of all, in a Christian spiritual position, coaching allows an individual to hear from the Holy Spirit and activate a plan of action in fulfilling the calling on one's life here and now.

Coaching initiatives in a faith-based organization lead to development. Faith-based leaders of organizations must recognize coaching has benefits, has values, and is needed, especially if there is a desire to grow more servant leaders. As a faith-based leader, you may question why coaching is vital in the church. Coaching is a jewel with brilliance and clarity toward which many organizations are beginning to gravitate because it inspires learning and fosters development. Leadership is vital to any organization, but especially within the faith community, coaching adds another dimension to the capacity and experience of individuals who lead and serve.

There are thousands of articles and books answering the questions about what coaching is and why it is important, but for some reason, when the subject of coaching is broached in a faith-based organization, there is often silence or a stiff-arm approach. One repeated reply in opposition to coaching within this context is that there is no explicit mention of coaching in the Bible. Another is that we will pray about it and see if the Lord releases us to coach. Why is there a need to pray for release in developing others? Why is there a need to question whether one should move from where one is to where one ought to be? Coaching is important because it instigates an awareness of the different operating leadership styles, theories, and working cultural beliefs one has, and it improves creativity and innovative abilities within oneself (IBC).

Coaching focuses on specific goals and improves performances, behaviors, and actions. Coaching appears to be either simplistic or complex, but it is neither. Coaching requires sitting down and listening. Coaching is not telling people what and how to do something, it is not solving problems for others, and it is not focusing on the future; instead, coaching is making a plan.

WHY IS COACHING IMPORTANT?

Coaching psychology enhances performance in both professional and personal domains in a nonclinical environment and applying models of coaching grounded in a therapeutic basis. Organizations and people encounter change, which requires shifting. Coaching can cause a change in one's mind-set due to increased self-awareness and confidence, which moves one's situation from challenge to opportunity. Coaching is important because it is not a one-size-fits-all; it is a tailored approach that produces results and does not require years before its effects are visible. In a 2016 article in the *Journal of Management Development*, contributors Athanassios Mihiotis and Niki Argirou (2016) voiced an important observance: Coaching has immensely evolved during the past decades from merely a developmental practice to a developmental technique internationally. Coaching is important because it encompasses several concepts such as collaboration, a focus on results, and deliberate engagement. It partners a coachee with a trained individual who asks thought-provoking questions, releases significant potential, and maximizes individual performance.

Take into consideration that God ordains relationships. Some relationships are seasonal, some are for life, and some are just in passing. Perhaps a relationship is developed as a teaching moment. Coaching is relational; it is temporary and does not last forever. Ecclesiastes 3:1 says, "For everything, there is a season and a time for every matter under heaven" (ESV). This chapter in Ecclesiastes describes coaching and further stresses Solomon's teaching in the Old Testament regarding that which is temporary and that which is eternal. The tangible things of man are temporary, but the intangibles, which come from God, have a long-lasting impact; they are eternal.

COACHING SKILLS

Professional management coaches should master a number of skills when operating in a coaching capacity, whether secular or religious. Martha Duesterhoft (2015), along with Linda Miller and Chad Hall (2007), suggest the role of a coach is to ask various questions (instead of telling) and to focus on the individual performance issue. Coaches and the coaching profession are not designed to fix anyone. Rather, coaches set clear accountability and adjust, as needed, to provide teaching moments. Coaches need to be patient, supportive, perceptive, present (this means not preoccupied with the next question), others-aware, self-aware, knowledgeable, able to develop rapport, and able to identify the difference between a coaching-centered relationship and a mentoring or counseling relationship.

James Kouzes and Barry Posner (2012), the authors of *The Leadership Challenge*, suggest leaders instigate extraordinary events and performance through the process of transforming thoughts and behaviors. It is important to remember that leadership coaching skills require the coachee's participation, while the coach listens for trigger words or actions that lead to more significant interaction between the two. A coach is there to assist another with emerging in the gifts and talents given to him or her by God; these gifts are sharpened through knowledge, experience, education, expertise, and understanding. Coaching relationships are developed by working through processes and reaching milestones that change human behavior. Core competencies of the International Coach Federation (ICF) begin with setting the foundation. Joseph O'Connor and Andrea Lages (2004), contributors to the international coaching community, provide clarity regarding coaching as a powerful tool. They believe one's mind-set is changed when a specific plan is developed and when there is a reason for the desired change. The coaching process moves from infancy to adulthood as the project matures. Coaching is assisting an individual to change his/her behavior.

In the process of developing yourself, encountering the root of whatever issue you are confronting provides an eyebrow-arched aha moment. Think about this: Coaching is a unique process that includes sitting down and listening. Listening is considered one of the hardest things to do, yet it is essential to understanding another person. Proverbs 18:15 reminds us, "An intelligent heart acquires knowledge, and the ear of the wise seeks knowledge" (ESV). In the simplest terms, this means when you have the right information, you can make sound decisions because you have the facts. You are open to new possibilities, and you hear the perspective or theory of the other. This sometimes can be difficult to obtain, but thorough relationship understanding can be developed.

In summary, these varying definitions of coaching are committed to guiding individuals or groups through challenges while assisting them in moving forward with confidence, prompted by a mind-set change. While coaching as a faith-based leader, it's also important to keep in mind you are not counseling. (The difference between counseling and coaching will be covered later in the book.) Coaching is not a therapy to overcome previous influences from difficult circumstances of the past. Coaching is servant leadership because you are assisting individuals to build upon their calling, goals, and desires so they can move toward a better future—spiritually, personally, and professionally.

COACHING IS RELATIONAL

Coaching is relational; it requires development, rapport, and trust. A faith-based leader (i.e. Pastor) can develop rapport and trust with his or her designated leaders by spending time with them and explaining the relationship between the coach, the coachee, and the Holy Spirit. The Holy Spirit will guide and keep His purpose at the center as the coach and coachee interact. As the coach/coachee relationship develops, results will occur as a natural result of the process of active listening and asking powerful, thought-provoking questions.

A trusted relationship between the coach (faith-based leader) and the coachee begins in an inaugural stage. The person being coached will focus on where he or she is currently while identifying specific goals and visions, challenges, and opportunities. The coaching conversations lead to exposing core issues, developing plans to overcome barriers, discussing resources needed to reach the intended end state, and identifying strengths and weaknesses. The coach (faith-based leader) becomes the listening ear and helps the coachee prune, for the sake of growth, through a process of clarifying goals and purpose and developing a realistic strategy. The coachee sets and reaches goals, deepens his or her relationship with the coach (and, most important, with the Holy Spirit), and gains a spiritual balance, which has an enormous effect on his/her life, personally and professionally. The coaching process allows the coachee to move forward into his or her calling.

ASSESSMENTS

Assessments are ubiquitous and have been around for over two thousand years. The question is, however, what is the purpose of assessments? And how do you assess the strengths of leaders serving in different capacities and religious organizations? Assessments within Christian settings provide the spiritual leader (coach) and the coachee with an understanding of where he or she currently is as a result of the tool used to measure one's gifts or talents. Assessments are not used to argue an individual's calling. Assessments need to be conducted in religious settings or business organizations, which set the tone for coaching. Coaching requires a knowledge of the coachee's strengths and assisting him/her in capitalizing on those strengths to reach his/her maximum potential. It is important to understand the value and benefits as well as the reason for utilizing assessments within a religious setting.

In Exodus 18, Moses sent his wife and two sons back to her father's house, but Jethro returned his daughter and two grandsons to him when he was serving in the desert at the foot of Mount Sinai. Jethro, the priest of Midian, sat with Moses and delighted in all God was doing for the people of Israel after being delivered from the hands of the Egyptians and Pharaoh. Jethro witnessed, observed, and assessed Moses's labors, as judge for the people, from morning until evening and provided Moses with a solution that would keep him from wearing himself down, freeing him to handle other important matters. Moses took the wise counsel of Jethro, his father-in-law; he assessed and selected others to serve as leaders to judge issues.

An assessment is a tool that provides a coach with clear answers regarding the coachee, whether through a self-assessment, 360-degree assessment, performance-based assessment, knowledge-based assessment, or faith-based inventory/gifts assessment. A plethora of myths surround assessments, but it is important to remember an assessment is effective only when followed up with a clear explanation of the results. Research provided by Leni Wildflower and Diane Brennan (2011) concludes assessment data (self-reported or through multi-writer feedback or other means) provides an individual with new self-awareness and insights. Assessments serve in two ways: through the ability and through the language to articulate these new understandings. Assessment results are usually based on standards; the standards are what organizations have labeled as the norm for the industry. Galatians 6:3–4 reminds us, "For if anyone thinks he is something when he is nothing, he deceives himself. But let each one test his work, and then his reason to boast will be in himself and not in his neighbor" (ESV). In other words, no Christian should think he or she is independent and does not need help from others, and no one should feel excused from the task of helping others.

▌SERVANT LEADERSHIP

When we hear the term *servant leader,* many Christians think of Jesus the Christ, not Robert Greenleaf (2002), the pioneer who coined the term. Servant leadership is often described as placing the needs of others before self. This understanding of servant is referenced in Matthew's account of what Jesus tells James and John's mother in Matthew 20:28: "even as the Son of Man came not to be served but to serve, and to give His life as a ransom for many" (ESV).

Mary, Jesus's mother, had the definition of servant leadership correct when she talked to the angel who visited her. "And Mary said, 'Behold, I am the servant of the Lord: Let it be to me according to your word.' And the angel departed from her" (Luke 1:38 ESV). Mary's willing acceptance to serve is aligned with Robert Greenleaf's (2002) definition of servant leader as one who desires to take on the same demeanor, behavior, and attitude as those whom they serve. Faith-based leaders who understand what coaching is and the importance of coaching grasp the concept of being a servant leader in alignment with Robert Greenleaf's (2002) belief that the act of serving is a natural feeling in which one wants to serve first.

▌REFLECTION: WHAT DO I NEED?

I remember walking into my company commander's office in 1991 as a new second lieutenant, thinking to myself, *What is this going to be about?* I was new to the unit, so I knew I was still in-processing and I could not have violated anything yet. I cannot recall much, other than my commander saying that in the military, there are three things we do and do well: mentor, teach, and coach. I struggled because from my experience, teaching was hit-or-miss.

The mentoring I received was merely stories of how the individual had made it, and if I wanted success, I should follow suit. I listened, but he never asked me what my goals were. I was so detached from the session. I thought, *This is sad*, and I wanted out of the military because there was no personal development taking place. (From my foxhole, I thought I had made a mistake and wanted to go home.)

One commander left, and another commander took his place in the organization. With the new leader, things began to change. The new commander conducted leadership development sessions, and his teaching and mentoring was centered on being a great leader in the military. The new leader attempted to coach but not effectively; I compare his approach to that of an athletic coach, as he gave us all the plays (directives) regarding how we needed to maneuver through our career, down to the specifics of where he thought we should ask our assignment manager to send us when it came to our next military assignment. I ignored his advice. Although he had plenty of advice, he never asked me what my goals were outside of the military. I did not want to be like either of these two commanders because, in my opinion, they did not understand the trifecta of teaching, mentoring, and coaching.

Catapult to 1993. I was now at a new duty station, and the new commander called me in for an initial meeting. When I asked him to be my mentor, he looked at me and said, "I do not think it works that way; I select whom I desire to mentor." He had no intention or desire to serve me in this capacity. For many years I carried a belief that I could not rely on others to assist me to reach my goals. Having not been exposed to coaching at this time, I thought I would simply take care of myself. Throughout my twenty-three years in the military, even as an officer, I unfortunately was required to rely on self-guidance to meet my professional and personal goals.

TAKEAWAYS

Leaders must understand coaching is the art and the practice of enabling individuals and groups to traverse from where they are in the present to where they desire to move forward. Coaching involves a trained individual who understands the art and science of how to guide individuals to increased potential and possibilities. The coachee develops greater confidence, becomes more committed, and becomes even more courageous while working to achieve his/her goals. Coaching is not merely providing answers to an individual (coachee); instead, coaching is empowering him/her to discover what he/she has allowed to lay dormant in his/her life. The coachee begins to develop and design a plan of action to bring the goal or desire into reality. Stoltzfus (2005) describes leadership coaching in this manner: Coaching is the practice of believing in people, so it empowers them to change. Coaches are change experts who are skilled in assisting others in taking control of their lives, with the intent to act in maximizing one's perspective.

CHAPTER 2
The Coaching Relationship

Trust in the Lord with all your heart, and do not lean on
your own understanding. In all your ways acknowledge
him, and he will make straight your paths.
—Proverbs 3:5–5 (ESV)

How do you effectively engage a potential organization
or individual, with the intent of positively influencing
performance and decision-making processes? The key to impacting
organizational or individual improvement is centered in authentic
relationships, especially within the coaching context. When
engaging in a coaching relationship, developing a relationship with
the coachee must be the primary goal.

I remember listening to a podcast from the Center of Creative
Leadership on "The Coaching Relationship," and the speaker
reminded listeners of an important point: What works for one coach
may not work for another, and a coaching relationship requires the
right fit to be successful. As a coach, I believe the first coaching
engagement meeting is not enough to provide me information for
building a relationship with a coachee. It requires time to develop
a connection, as well as a strong alignment of values. Let's look at
establishing the coaching relationship in the same way you would
any other relationship; there must first be an attraction or chemistry
between the two individuals. I'm not referring to a physical attraction
but an attraction to serve and support the coachee from a place of
being stuck to a place of effectiveness. When one is stuck, he/she is

unable to find a solution for moving forward on his/her own. The coaching relationship is the key to developing the tools necessary to move from where the person is currently to the place, he/she desires to be. An authentic relationship is key to facilitating this process. In this chapter, we will discuss the essentials necessary for effectively establishing a coaching relationship. When initiating the coaching relationship, four specific elements need to be considered:

1. Session format (location of appointments, whether in person or online)
2. Scheduling appointments (timing/frequency)
3. Confidentiality agreement
4. Handling payments (when applicable)

Three of the four areas above are also in alignment with the ICF core competency model for coaching. Other critical areas within this model are establishing clear assumptions, clarifying expectations and exploring issues, how coaching is a partnership, and how to sustain a coaching relationship. I want to focus on establishing the coaching relationship. This requires the development of trust and intimacy with the client and having an apparent coaching presence.

ESTABLISHING THE COACHING RELATIONSHIP AND EXPLORING ISSUES

Relationship building is the catalyst for successful coaching. Henry Kimsey-House, Karen Kimsey-House, Phillip Sandahl, and Laura Whitworth (2011), the authors of *Co-Active Coaching: Changing Business and Transforming Lives*, remind readers, "Coaching is not so much a methodology as it is a relationship … the real art of effective coaching comes from the coach's ability to work within the context of the relationship" (15). Kimsey-House, et al., believe every coachee is unique, and it is important to get to know the individual's nuances, which is beneficial in understanding his/her fitness for coaching. When building a coaching relationship, it is important to first pray for guidance; then, once engaged as a leader or coach, there is a need for an agreement. Coaching occurs when the coach and coachee connect and agree, which leads to a partnership and flourishes a relationship. There are many factors to consider when building a coaching relationship. First, there is a need to ensure the coachee is receptive to and desires the coaching relationship. Without such receptivity, any coaching activity will be fruitless. Second, find out if an assessment has been conducted. This provides background information and is helpful in understanding the organizational culture or where the individual is personally in regard to certain areas of leadership development. Exploring issues in coaching requires the ability to unearth the root issue of a particular area of concern. The coaching process uncovers these underlying issues, which are connected to decisions and goals. Dr. Gary Collins (2002) recommends the following four questions when issues arise in coaching engagements: (1) How might coaching be useful? (2) Where are you now? (3) How would you like things to be different? (4) What will get in the way? (90–91). These four questions are also helpful when initially engaging clients and assessing their readiness for a coaching relationship.

The coaching relationship is launched once the desire to be coached is established and an agreement is in place. As the coach and coachee meet, the relationship will form, leading to transformation for the coachee (as well as for the coach). In the beginning, one of the best methods for stimulating productive conversation is by asking questions. Asking powerful questions is a core practice at the heart of the coaching profession. When I am discussing the potential of a coaching relationship with a prospective client, I ask powerful questions to identify opportunities for growth.

When it comes to developing a coaching relationship with others, there are specific factors to consider:

- begin with an agreement
- build a relationship
- understand the coachee's initial assumptions

- explore issues with the coachee
- sustain the coaching relationship through candid communication.

Great coaching relationships are authentic and unconditional, and they do not simply or arbitrarily happen outside of intentional and self-disclosing communication. Think of an authentic relationship as one having no shame, hiding, or façade. In contrast, when this type of authenticity is not present in a coaching relationship, it most assuredly leads to a lack of transparency, which develops roadblocks in making authentic progress in areas of growth. As coaches, opportunities may arise to set the tone by modeling transparency for our coachees in an area of personal significance. Share about a goal you had and struggled to meet. Avoid generalizing and show your human side. When you set the example by stepping out first in transparency, it allows the coachee to feel safe and willing to open up and talk. This comes with a small caveat: Within the right context, this is effective and powerful, but be careful not to reveal too much than is helpful and maintain a level of professionalism.

When there is authenticity in a coaching relationship, there is transparency and honesty. This leads the way to unconditional coaching. Unconditional coaching is a coaching relationship free from judgment and demonstrated by one's ability to listen actively, ask compelling questions, and communicate in a manner that extracts answers and assists the coachee in reaching goals. Unconditional coaching is acceptance and belief in the coachee and further demonstrates the agape love described in 2 Corinthians 5:16: "From now on, therefore, we regard no one according to the flesh. Even though we once regarded Christ according to the flesh, we regard him thus no longer" (ESV). Unconditional coaching requires a keen awareness of the preeminence of the coachee's agenda and interests. It is a belief this relationship is not about you or how you feel about the issues but rather how to best help the coachee get where he/she seeks to go. It is important to lay aside anything that hinders the coachee's time. As professional coaches and as leaders, we must learn to recognize when our emotions are getting in the way and, when necessary, reschedule for the sake of the coachee and self when personal feelings are likely to interfere or disrupt the professionalism of the coaching engagement. When considering the value of authentic relationships in the coaching relationship, here are questions you must ask yourself:

- As a leader, how important are relationships to you?
- What happens when the coaching relationship is strained?
- What happens when there is deception?
- What happens to the relationship if the other party is not interested in being further engaged?
- When do you, as a leader, know there are uncertainties as well as a lack of disclosure?

These questions are powerful considerations for you to ponder and use as a personal examination tool. They help you to reflect on what relationships mean and the effectiveness and essentiality of two parties when working toward a common goal. The questions are also a means to measure how vested you are in serving others. The foundation in coaching begins with building a relationship and motivating the coachee.

Pioneer Christian coach Tony Stoltzfus (2005) believes when an individual seeks out a coaching relationship, chances are the person is motivated. Stoltzfus also suggests you evaluate the motivation of the interested individual with simple questions, such as:

- What piqued your interest in coaching?
- How will reaching your goal change your life?
- What do you expect out of the coaching relationship?
- What are the goals you would like to work on?
- How motivated are you to reach your objectives? (100–101)

There are no right or wrong answers to these questions; the intent is to listen to the desire of the potential coachee, as this helps with engaging his or her motivation, and it is foundational in building a coaching relationship. Consider Figure 1, the Coaching Relationship. This highlights an important and vital part of coaching. Coaching is about the relationship, creating an environment, and being present. In order to establish a coaching presence, your initial engagement meeting is recommended to be twice as long as a regular engagement to allow time to develop a relational foundation. If at all possible, this initial meeting should take place in person. Remember the goal is to listen, watch, and establish a level of comfort as a means of breaking the ice in the relationship. This introductory meeting also provides you, as the coach, with the information you need that cannot be learned from the intake form. This initial engagement is instrumental in establishing rapport. Relational deal-breakers occur when there is a lack of respect, honesty, and—most important—trust. In a coaching relationship, a dire need exists to ensure the coachee is comfortable when discussing areas of growth. In such an environment, doors open and a partnership that facilitates healing begins.

While scanning and streamlining the plethora of books written on coaching, my initial inquiries were to find topics on the importance of the coaching relationship. After countless hours combing through the collection of books in my library and online, I realized there is a severe lack of resources to address one the most important and foundational steps in coaching: establishing a coaching relationship. Perhaps my scope and research approach were too narrow. Yet at this juncture, the Holy Spirit reminded me to first stop and examine my relationship with Him. I sat down and thought back to when I learned how to trust God and, as a result, others. Through learning how to trust God, I gained the ability to be honest and vulnerable with others and to share my struggles with others for the sake of improving. This process has led me to significant personal growth. This same concept translates to the initiation of a coaching relationship. Solomon, the author of Proverbs, provided teaching to help others attain wisdom, to be a disciple, and to live prudently in his or her daily life. Proverbs 3:5–6 teaches believers, "Trust in the Lord with all your heart, and do not lean on your own understanding. In all your ways acknowledge him, and he will make straight your paths" (ESV). Coaching requires faith and trust while partnering and disclosing information.

As a leader, it is important to remember, when serving in the capacity of a coach or when an external coach is engaging with a coachee, the goal is a safe place to find direction and purpose and obtain a more significant meaning for life purpose and direction. The coaching relationship reveals strengths, weaknesses, fears, and failures, but before that can occur, trust must be established. In a coaching relationship, it is the coach's responsibility to guard the private information of the coachee, whether verbal or written. As a faith-based or business leader, it is important to remember coaching relationships do not occur overnight; patience is paramount during the relationship-building process. Gary Collins, the author of *Christian Coaching* (2002), references four areas that are critical in relationship building: partnership, clear assumptions, exploring issues, and the coaching agreement. Collins further believes "the coach must take the lead in connecting with the client, building rapport and establishing a solid relationship" (83). The ICF established core competencies that include setting the foundation, co-creating the relationship, efficiently communicating, and facilitating learning and results. These competencies are continuous throughout coaching engagements. Consider any influential person in your life who assisted you in reaching your goals; this is an example of a basic coaching relationship. The coaching relationship at any level has the potential to be influential and life-changing. Tony Stoltzfus (2005) leaves a reassuring thought pertaining to a coaching relationship: "It is an extraordinary relationship. It's an investment in another person which allows them to honestly say, it made a difference having someone believe in me" (88).

ESTABLISH CLEAR ASSUMPTIONS AND CLARIFY EXPECTATIONS

Once the coaching relationship is established and rapport is growing, it is important to ensure there are clear expectations and that the coachee clearly understands what is expected in the coaching

COACHING IS SERVANT LEADERSHIP

partnership. There is nothing worse than false assumptions and fogged expectations in a coaching relationship, and it is important to evaluate and ask questions from time to time to watch for the possibility of any uncertainties that may form. It is essential to talk about what the coachee expects for the sake of managing expectations and dispelling assumptions about what coaching will and will not do or is about. Kimsey-House, et al. (2011), clearly reminds readers that the skills for clarifying are listening, asking questions, and reframing. This is a part of the step in co-creating the relationship after setting the foundation. In this process, a coach or leader assesses the readiness of an individual for coaching. Evaluating the readiness of a coachee is different from conducting assessments. (Assessments are covered in chapter 3.) Readiness is defined as one who is prepared and disposed to participating in a profitable coaching relationship. To assess the readiness of a coachee, *Adaptive Coaching* by Terry R. Bacon and Karen Spear (2003) provides beneficial tools (this book may not fit every coach) that identify readiness factors and indicators of high, medium, and low. A high readiness indicator signifies high favorability for the coaching relationship to be successful in helping the coachee meet his/her goals.

Coaching signifies different ideas to different individuals, and therefore, it is important to clarify alignment of goals and expectations. When a coachee, whether faith-based or non–faith-based, engages in coaching, ask him or her a simple two-part question: (1) What are you expecting from this partnership? (2) Why is this expectation important to you?

As a coach, this accomplishes two objectives. First, it provides a glimpse into the expectations of the coachee. Second, it helps the coach understand why coaching is important to what the coachee desires to accomplish. I recommend outlining clear, written expectations; this is a productive tool as well as a reminder to the coachee of the significance and professionalism associated with coaching. (This is not a practice of every coach, but such a document can help serve as accountability and ensure clarity of goals.) As a leader, it is important to clarify what is important as well as what others expect, as both affect performance and behavior.

When coachees trust you as their coach, in time they will grow in transparency, which leads to full disclosure. The International Coach Federation (ICF) identifies trust and establishing an agreement as vital components to setting the foundation in coaching. Trust alone is a complicated process that involves many factors, such as cost, personal vulnerabilities, and uncertainties of the future. The formerly mentioned practices of clarifying assumptions and expectations, as well as building trust, are important because of the vulnerability of the coachee during the process of disclosure. Professors Jovana Markovic, Jean McAtavey, and Priva Fischweicher (2014) of Barry University (Florida) define the construct of trust in regard to coaching "as an individual's willingness to become vulnerable to another individual with some hope of a positive outcome" (104). They believe trust has two foundations: (1) cognitive trust formed from evidence, and (2) affective trust associated with emotions.

Leaders in faith-based and non–faith-based organizations alike who understand how relationships work also know a coaching relationship among staff members can further strengthen individual leadership skills and assist in better decision-making processes, as coaching is a teaching tool that leads to results. Such effectiveness only exists, however, when there is trust, establishment of clear assumptions, and managed expectations.

REFLECTION: TRUST AN AWAKENING AND BEGINNING OF A RELATIONSHIP

In the late '80s, I was a college freshman in Norfolk, Virginia. I had two other roommates, and we lived in a small, cramped high-rise dormitory. One night I had a dream I was leaning out of the window of the dorm. In this dream, Jesus extended his hand, and I heard a voice telling me to "come." I remember looking at Jesus and then looked down and said, "I do not want to fall because there is nothing beneath me." I did not know what to make of the situation because Jesus did not talk, but the voice (the Holy Spirit) was giving me instructions. I was standing on the ledge in the window, but I did not move toward Jesus. I heard, "Do you trust the Father?" I said no, because fathers disappoint and do not keep their promises, just like my father did not keep his promises. The voice said, "I am not your natural father. I will take care of you, but first you must trust me." I waited, and then I walked out to Jesus's hand without fear or doubt. When I woke up, my roommates had already left for class. From that day, allowing myself to trust others was no longer an issue. My dream awakened me to the meaning of trust and showed me how important it is to let go of the past in order to live a freer life. I had been allowing what my biological father did to me as a child continue to affect my young adulthood in many areas of my life. As a result, my relationships with others had become strained or doubtful. I initially did not know what to make of the dream because I had been a believer since the age of thirteen and had been baptized. I didn't realize I needed to learn to trust. That dream changed my life, however, and I wanted to have an even closer relationship with the Lord and more trusting relationships with others.

THE COACHING AGREEMENT

> Two are better than one because they have
> a good reward for their toil.
> —Ecclesiastes 4:9 (ESV)

Ecclesiastes 4:9 teaches us the advantages of cooperating with others. Life is designed for companionship. Partnering with another is also a form of trust and proves we are not here to be alone but to serve others. How many times in a day is the word *agreement* heard around the world, and how many times, when there is a breach of agreement, does confusion and disagreement emerge in strife? In a coaching relationship, it is better to develop clear expectations and parameters than to merely wait it out or play it by ear. Every coaching relationship should have a coaching agreement. A coaching agreement sets the tone for a professional relationship and establishes roles and responsibilities of the coach and coachee. ICF suggests that when setting the foundation for coaching, the coaching agreement provides the coachee the process and context for the relationship. The need for a contract also protects both parties in the event of a breach of confidentiality or sharing materials intended only for the coachee.

Christian coach Tony Stoltzfus (2005) highlights how agreements nurture accountability. Accountability helps coachees take the coaching relationship more seriously, and, in turn, there is greater success. Christian coach Gary Collins (2002) emphasizes coaching is not as formal as the therapist/patient relationship; it is rather more of a partnership. The difference between the coach and the coachee is that one has the skills, perspective, and experience that is useful to the other. In his book *Christian Coaching*, Collins pens this message regarding two of the core competencies of coaching: "Clients and coaches need to work together in a partnership that gets things done in the present and clarifies how present learning can be applied in the future" (28). Coaching is partnership with a purpose that causes movement toward desired realistic goals.

▎SUSTAINING A COACHING RELATIONSHIP

Coaching relationships are sustained through the application of coaching skills and include listening, questioning, and responding, as well as recognizing and understanding the learning style of the coachee. Lorri Freifeld (2012), a contributing writer for Training. com, believes coaches who realize how a coachee learns reach a higher rate of successful transferring of capabilities. Freifeld suggests there are six steps to sustaining a coaching relationship:

1. Verify the context of the coaching assignment and clarify expectations.
2. Establish a coaching partnership after reviewing the coachee's data (records).

COACHING IS SERVANT LEADERSHIP

3. Create a realistic coaching plan.
4. Coach as well as serve as a thinking partner.
5. Assess results from processes.
6. Identify steps and share essential learning.

Coaching has many recommended phases, stages, and methods, but it will not have success or occur if the coach and coachee are not communicating effectively. Active listening requires focusing on what is and is not being said and reading expressions from the context of the conversation. First, coaching relationships are sustainable only when the roles and responsibilities of the coach and coachee are understood and there is honesty as well as an established sense of safety. Second, the partnership must be transparent, with the coach and coachee working together toward the agenda of the coachee. Third, when creating the coaching plan, remember the coachee's areas of interest and concern are paramount. While it is the coachee's agenda, you, as the coach, are responsible for the length of time, the frequency of meeting, and challenging the coachee by asking powerful questions. Fourth, remain in the partnership model; coaches do not tell coachees what to do. The role of the coach is to be intentional and be a thinking partner. Fifth, assess the results and ensure you, as the coach, are facilitating learning and growth. Coaching becomes effective through creating awareness and creating opportunities for the coachee to learn and be held accountable to accomplish his/her goals. Finally, the coach leverages outcomes and ensures the coachee is working in alignment with organizational goals (when applicable).

Why is it important for the leader to emphasize the importance of relationships in coaching? Leaders must remember not everyone is ready for a coaching relationship. For a coachee to move from where he or she is toward achieving a goal requires time and motivation, as well as trust and vulnerability. If there is a desire to improve his or her performance and/or behavior, then motivation will be a driving factor. Leaders must understand that occasionally, after an initial readiness review, a coach will provide feedback that indicates an individual may not be a suitable candidate for coaching at the current time. Leaders, it is important to think back to what *relationship* means and its effects. The coaching relationship actually has an inception before the first meeting ever takes place; it starts in the heart of the coachee and develops from there. Coaching relationships possess the right foundation when the coachee feels he or she can trust the coach, feels safe, and is clear on the coaching agreement, which keeps both parties accountable. The coaching engagements are client-driven. It is also important for leaders to remember that establishing trust and intimacy takes time.

TAKEAWAYS

Relationship-building is the catalyst for successful coaching. The coaching relationship is launched once the desire to be coached is established. The relationship process does not happen overnight; it takes time. The goals in launching a successful coaching relationship to are to create a safe place for the coachee, provide clear direction on the importance of being accountable for one's actions, and discuss purpose and goals. After time passes and the relationship is forming, establish clear assumptions and clarify expectations, which eliminates the pitfalls of vagueness. The coaching agreement is also an important part of the coaching relationship because it provides the coach with answers and assists in developing the coachee. Coaching relationships are sustained through the application of coaching skills and in a context with a clear understanding of the roles and responsibilities of the coach and coachee.

CHAPTER 3
The Value and Use of Assessments in Coaching

> Now when Jesus came into the district of Caesarea Philippi,
> he asked his disciples, "Who do people say that the Son of
> Man is?" And they said, "Some say John the Baptist, others
> say Elijah, and others Jeremiah or one of the prophets."
> He said to them, "But who do you say that I am?"
> —Matthew 16:13–15 (ESV)

How many books have you read that talk explicitly about assessments or surveys, and of these, how many of them left you with lack of clarity or understanding? The concept of assessments or surveys often feels daunting and elicits feelings of confusion, or peril. Regardless of what you may have experienced, assessments are not as daunting as they appear! Why is the word *assessments* often associated with an adverse report or an unwanted matter? As a person who has endured a battery of assessments throughout my career, I fully understand the feeling. But my experiences have taught me to relax and remember it is merely an assessment, not a test of my own worth. When defining the word assessment, think of a valuation of a particular area. Assessments can serve as a valuable tool within the coaching context.

Terry Bacon and Karen Spear (2003), the authors of *Adaptive Coaching: The Art and Practice of a Client-Centered Approach to Performance Improvement*, stress valid points about the assessment practice: Gathering information through an assessment is an excellent tool for providing baseline data from others or self, and feedback from assessments provides a snapshot of awareness, perceptions, strengths, and weaknesses that are usually identified through emotional intelligence (this is paramount when building teams). The most effective questions in assessments target two areas: skills and behavior. This chapter will assist in discovery or rediscovery of how leadership assessments are essential to growing and coaching.

The organization that decides to implement assessments, internally or externally, must have a clear purpose for its assessments and, while preparing for assessments, be able to identify what information will serve the overall mission and goals of both the organization and the individual. Organizations must also recognize there are different types of assessments; how to determine which will be most beneficial is key. Leaders desiring to administer an assessment must understand one size does not fit all; more important, it is critical to employ the right assessment instrument to attain one's desired outcome. The feedback gleaned from the correct assessment can have a significant impact on an individual or organization seeking growth and change. According to the authors of *The Handbook of Leadership Development*, Ellen Van Velsor, Cynthia McCauley, and Marion Ruderman (2010), feedback from assessments provides participants with a picture of their current effectiveness and provides benchmarks for planning. Table 1 provides a list of assessments to consider in coaching and leadership. The discussion in this chapter, however, will primarily focus on 360-degree assessments and feedback as a significant tool in the coaching context.

According to Marshall Goldsmith (2007), the author of *What Got You Here, Won't Get You There,* feedback has been around since the first man saw his reflection in the water when bending down to take a drink. Since the first initial feedback, assessments have developed into powerful and complex tools to impact lives through clarifying one's current state and what is needed for further growth in myriad areas. When a leader seeks a coach for the purpose of personal and professional growth, a well-executed assessment will be a powerful tool for the potential coach to identify how to best engage this leader. Authors Leni Wildflower and Diane Brennan (2011) support the suggestion that assessments have the propensity to be an effective and efficient method of informing the client and the coach about preferences, styles, skills, and abilities that advance the coaching processes. The premise is also correct for organizations that are experienced and knowledgeable with assessments. Data from assessments provide an individual with a new self-awareness and insight, as well as a language that articulates a more modern understanding regarding feedback.

When I thought about what is important in and for developing others, it dawned on me that there is a need to stress how vital wise counsel is indispensable for growth and development. In chapter 1, I stated that coaching is not counseling. The counsel I refer to in this section comes from a biblical context regarding feedback from assessments, not as a counselor per se. Feedback from assessments should assist in developing the coachee and stimulating growth. In chapter 2, I mentioned the need to assess a coachee's readiness; this is not the same type of assessment that reveals self-awareness and strengths. I firmly believe when an individual knows himself well and works with a coach to develop a plan of action to address challenge areas to reach desired goals, the winners are both the organization and the individual.

In the process of developing leaders within the coaching context, having the right data about an individual, an organization, and the future of an organization is an excellent and tangible tool in the decision-making process. I think of assessments as information that paints a picture or provides a perception of an individual for the purpose of facilitating growth.

PURPOSE AND PREPARING FOR ASSESSMENTS

The further leaders advance in their roles, the more detached they can become from honest feedback. The purpose of an assessment is to provide this honest feedback while focusing on strengths, just as the objective of coaching is to be a thinking partner.

Wildflower and Brennan (2011), the authors of *The Handbook of Knowledge-Based Coaching*, support the notion that an assessment is as effective as the coaching discussions that occur afterward. As a coach, after assessing one's readiness for coaching, I ask individuals to undergo an assessment for the purpose of developing a baseline understanding of their current state and areas of needed growth. If there is resistance, I explore the why, as this can also be significant. Whenever a coach communicates the need for an assessment, he or she needs to be able to share the following: why an assessment is necessary, which assessment is recommended, when the assessment will be administered, and most importantly, how the assessment will be conducted. This will help provide reassurance and context for the coachee to cooperate with the process. Adequately preparing individuals for assessments is a way to ease the difficulty that some perceive as surrounding an assessment. As a leader, your role is significant in helping to alleviate tension and apprehension by clearly communicating expectations. Although an assessment is not a test, some still perceive it as such and may suffer from performance anxiety, which can hinder the process. Ryan Smith, the author of the article "5 Ways to Prepare Employees For 360-Degree Feedback," believes there are effective ways to prepare individuals to experience effective feedback from assessments. The five ways to prepare others for feedback are as follows:

1. Define the measurement objectives by asking the following questions:
    a. What skills are necessary to the organization?
    b. How will we measure them and what will I do with the data?
    c. Who in particular are we going to evaluate?
2. Communicate the purpose of the assessment. This will alleviate a number of uncertainties and ambiguity. If the reason for conducting the assessment is not apparent, confusion, fear, and doubt may creep in, as individuals

are concerned with how they are perceived and how such information about them will be used.

3. State your expectations. Use this opportunity to give a refresher on how the process works and to set expectations.

4. Clarify who will have access to the assessment results. Information disclosure allows the coachee to know who will see the feedback and whether it will be distributed or anonymous.

5. Despite all of your best efforts to prepare your individuals for the 360-degree feedback process, individuals still may experience some anxiety. A way to dispel uneasy feelings is by establishing an open forum for questions before, during, and after the reviews. By establishing a safe and open forum to discuss questions and concerns, you give participants a voice. This is a critical differentiator and creates buy-in, making them more receptive to the feedback they receive.

One of the most challenging aspects of any 360-degree feedback process is motivating individuals to complete the evaluations. As noted, clearly outlining expectations will help facilitate the process. The feedback delivered is a foundational planning tool; the information gleaned provides clarity for identifying areas of growth. Jack Zenger (2016), the author of *How Effective Are Your 360-Degree Feedback Assessments?*, believes individuals become increasingly more comfortable receiving feedback when delivery is constant and when there is an understanding the feedback is centered on focusing on strengths.

▎WISE COUNSEL (ASSESSMENTS)

As a Christian coach and one who has served in several leadership positions in the church, I firmly believe it is crucial for leaders to know what their strengths and weaknesses are and seek ways to improve. Feedback from wise counsel provides individuals with the truth about their performances and behaviors, which is instrumental in keeping them from derailing. When determining coaching relationships, leaders in a religious organization should take into consideration the individuals who support the organizational vision, mission, and goals and gravitate toward providing wise counsel to those serving. Wise counsel comes when Christian leaders consider the teachings of Proverbs, 2 Timothy, and Colossians. Individuals who are believers must pray for God's guidance in finding the right person to assist in his or her growth and development. It is essential to find a person of wisdom who is considered as a coach or mentor to provide honest feedback. Proverbs 1:7 reads, "The fear of the LORD is the beginning of knowledge; fools despise wisdom and instruction" (ESV). The Proverbs teach knowledge is important, regardless of one's position, and is practical for daily living.

Theologians John Walvoord and Roy Zuck (2004), the authors of *The Bible Knowledge Commentary Old Testament Edition*, suggest there are two approaches a man can adopt. The first is a way that is foolish to the things he is doing and to continue to walk in ways that lead to destruction because he does not believe there is a need for correction. The second way is to gain spiritual knowledge and correct his former behavior, which leads to wisdom. A wise (prudent) individual is open to constructive feedback and ensures he or she adjusts current behavior and performances based on assessments.

Contemporary leadership development understands the need to provide individuals with feedback. The various forms of feedback are collected from assessment sources, and a developmental plan is formulated to assist in changing one's current performance and behaviors. Any individual who fails to adhere to recommendations for improvement runs the risk of not being fully developed as a leader, team, or an organization. Proverbs 12:15 provides a timeless truth that teaches individuals what to do to avoid self-derailment: "The way of a fool is right in his own eyes, but a wise man listens to advice" (ESV).

Proverbs 15:22 states, "Without counsel plans fail, but with many advisers, they succeed" (ESV). Throughout Proverbs, there is a focus on the importance of obtaining advice from other trusted individuals about one's plans. As a leader, it is not advisable to remain fixated on thinking one way; it leads to missing wise counsel (feedback) that can change outcomes when adjustments are made. Leadership development plans provide direction, alignment, and commitment to facilitate growth and development. Feedback intensive programs (FIPs) assist in developing plans to prepare leaders, teams, and organizations to move to a higher level of responsibility. FIPs require discipline in accomplishing the work required. Once assessment results are collected and face-to-face counseling occurs, an individual is left to work on obtaining success in the areas assessed as weaknesses and on filling gaps.

Second Timothy 2:15 says, "Do your best to present yourself to God as one approved, a worker who does not need to be ashamed, rightly handling the word of truth" (ESV). Paul writes to Timothy to stay attentive and focus on his life and ministry. Christians often look for approval from men, but what Paul tells Timothy is not to seek approval of men but rather from God. Timothy is instructed to not pursue man's approval in winning a popularity contest but to be faithful and diligent in the ministry he has been given. Leaders experience humiliation when they are found doing their job poorly. Leaders experience reward when their honest hard work pays off. Contemporary leadership development feedback-intensive programs cause individuals to conduct self-assessments based on their experiences, prior training, and skills, which become the individuals' benchmarks. Feedback from others, then, primarily focuses on the individual's behavior, social skills, and identity, as well as empathy when working with others. Feedback-intensive programs challenge individuals to reach beyond their comfort zones and current awareness and prepare them for superior accomplishments.

"Whatever you do, work heartily, as for the Lord and not for men, knowing that from the Lord you will receive the inheritance as your reward. You are serving the Lord Christ" (Colossians 3:23–24 ESV). Paul writes to the Colossians about having a godly attitude and motive when rendering service to others. We should work for a higher cause. For example, we receive rewards for doing an excellent job for our employers. The Christian's attitude and motivation, however, should not be the accolades from superiors but in working for the Lord, which is a higher standard of performance and motivation with greater gratification and reward.

Contemporary leadership development focuses on developing others. James Kouzes and Barry Posner (2012), the authors of *Leadership Challenge*, challenge leaders to develop those around them by sharing the vision, enabling them and challenging them to establish and reach their goals. Feedback from an assessment is a conduit to encouraging and developing leaders. Leaders who work for the sake of others are also serving God through empowering and celebrating the achievements of individuals.

LEADERSHIP ASSESSMENTS

Who do people say that I am, and who do you say that I am? This is a question Jesus asked the disciples in Matthew 16:13–15. I believe Jesus already knew the answer, but He still desired to have feedback regarding the perception of others and then from the twelve men who were with him all the time. This question posed by Jesus is an example of what we should consider an assessment. Remember it is not a test; rather, it is an observation based on several benchmarks, such as performance and behavior. Leadership assessment tools do not all measure the same areas; the various types each has a primary focus. You can search the internet, triage books, or pray about the best assessment to meet your desired outcome. Authors Leni Wildflower and Diane Brennan (2011) provide a helpful review of potential assessments to consider (listed in table 1). Although certainly not an exhaustive list, the table contains a list of assessments for potential use. Wildflower and Brennan also remind readers that once results from an assessment are received and discussed, this is the point in which real coaching begins. The purpose of the assessment is to successfully facilitate and fuel the coaching process. Results from assessments assist coaches in deciding which coaching approach or style is instrumental or beneficial for the stable coaching relationship. Organizational leaders also should consider whether they will bring in an external coach to assist individuals and make this a part of a leadership development program once assessment results are returned to the organization. It bears repeating: Assessments may be new to an individual or taken years ago and he or she does not remember the results. In either situation, the results must be discussed. Regardless of how results are delivered, individuals may receive feedback from assessments in varying ways, and a leader or coach should be prepared. Some will receive these results positively, while others will receive them negatively, due to fear or other concerns. Regardless of the response, the coach or organizational leader can assist in guiding dialogue from the results into a positive opportunity for learning and growth.

Two effective, globally used assessments are the Myers-Brigg Type Indicator personality assessment (MBTI) and the 360-degree assessment, which gleans anonymous qualitative feedback on leaders from others within their spheres of influence. These two multi-sourced assessment instruments serve two purposes: (1) provide data regarding performance and behavior, which usually focuses on strengths, and (2) identify your personality type based on indicators. The 360-degree assessment has many advantages but can lead to mistakes during implementation if not administered correctly. Authors Scott Wimer and Kenneth Nowack (2006) of 13 *Common Mistakes When Using 360-Degree Feedback* identify these as follows:

1. Having no apparent purpose
2. Using it as a substitute
3. Not conducting a pilot test
4. Not involving key stakeholders
5. Having insufficient communication
6. Compromising confidentiality
7. Not making the use of the feedback clear
8. Not giving people sufficient resources
9. Not clarifying who owns the feedback
10. Having unfriendly administration and scoring

11. Linking to existing systems without a pilot
12. Making it an event rather than a process
13. Not evaluating effectiveness

Before, during, and after any assessment, Weimer and Nowack (2006) suggest you prepare yourself for questions or comments that need addressing. Being prepared for the feedback process is not insinuating you must be an expert in every area, but that careful consideration is taken in the method, and there is an openness for discussion. A leader who is ready to dialogue demonstrates he or she is also invested and engaged in the process. There are noted commonalities relating to successes and failures when there are concerns. Organizations armed with information from lessons learned and best practices are in a better position to avoid these common mistakes.

▌TYPES OF ASSESSMENTS

When considering what type of assessment to use in a particular scenario, ask how the data will be used. With thousands of assessments available, it is certainly essential to ensure the correct type of assessment is being administered for the specific context and objectives. As a former military officer, I participated in a 360-degree assessment every year, which led to an annual rating, and other assessments almost monthly for the sake of providing feedback for others. During this time, I developed a keen understanding of the 360-degree assessment and how it works. I grew to appreciate its significant benefits for leadership development and coaching. Another such instrument that yields significant impact for its users is the Myers-Briggs MBTI. "For as in one body we have many members, and the members do not all have the same function ..." (Romans 12: ESV). It is important to remember that although we are individuals, our differences are significant in regard to the end result. When working together toward the same goal and when considering personalities and behavior, feedback from a MBTI helps to consider who is the best person as the lead, as well as the best person to close the project when there are partnering tasks.

Not all assessments are the same. When pondering which one to use, consider empirical research, and if at all possible, avoid group decisions based on opinions and likes. Assessments should take no more than fifteen minutes to complete. Once results are in hand, this data provides coaches and leaders with the hypotheses to assist in boosting forward movement. Once data is gathered, prepare the feedback for delivery. Delivering feedback can be tricky; this is why it is essential to ask the coachee if she or he has previously completed an assessment. The answer to the question is helpful and also prepares leaders or coaches to respond appropriately, based on feedback. Feedback should be delivered as quickly as possible once results are provided and should offer the assessed with a snapshot of the findings in comparison to averages. Averages provide clarification of what others in similar situations or demographics also scored. This is not a tactic of deception; it allows individuals to see how they scored among peers. As a reminder, the 360-degree feedback assessment provides an analysis for how individuals perceive themselves and how others perceive them through observation of experience, competencies, behaviors, knowledge, and their relationships. Assessments are designed to discover, focus, and magnify the leader's strengths. Feedback from assessments can be the cornerstones of leadership development programs.

Faith-based leaders who are aware of faith-based assessments must take into consideration how to administer the assessment and why, as well as who should be assessed. Once the results are returned, the leader must have a plan for leadership development based on these results. It is not enough to merely conduct the assessment. You must be ready to effectively use the information. Faith-based assessments and surveys accomplish two objectives: They help leaders grow spiritually, and they assist them in serving effectively. I have attended churches in which the assessment was given as soon as individuals joined or became partners (new catchphrase) within the church to ensure all people conducted a self-reflection and assessed their gifts and talents, according to what God has called them to do. Other churches, however, wait until one is selected for leadership before conducting a survey. There are many assessments for a religious organization, and it is essential to find the one that fits your specific desired outcomes.

▌THE VALUE AND BENEFITS OF ASSESSMENTS

As a leader, it is essential to understand and articulate to individuals in your organization the purpose of assessments. Assessments are valuable to faith-based and non–faith-based organizations alike; in both contexts, it can be difficult to communicate feedback verbally without a specific feedback tool. Assessments, however, are designed to be constructive in a confidential manner. In a coaching setting, assessments help in creating dialogue. The assessment is a great tool to deepen coaching engagements and for the coachee to develop plans. Results from assessments provide a more vivid picture of the assessed, which may have been difficult to identify otherwise. Value-add stems from the process of comparing how one perceives his/her skills, performance, or personality attributes with assessment results. There is a plethora of benefits in regard to assessments. Eight advantages of assessments include the following: (1) increase of self-awareness, (2) clarification of behavior patterns, (3) measurement of how things are supposed to be and what actually occurs, (4) promotion of dialogue, (5) improvement of working relationships, (6) encouragement of personal development, (7) increase in accountability, and (8) enhancement of performance.

John Keyser (2014) of *Common-Sense Leadership* believes the greatest benefit of a 360-degree leadership assessment is the learning. Respect is gained from others, future critical conversations that lead to improvement are cultivated, and truth and honesty are shared. Accuracy from the 360-degree feedback offers more than one point of view, and the anonymity provides a more honest and well-rounded look. Feedback from assessments also provide the assessed a more precise understanding of his or her performance, and it promotes openness, again, because of confidentiality. And finally, 360-degree feedback is especially valuable as it communicates and reinforces an organization's values.

REFLECTION: ASSESSMENTS ARE NOT TO BE TAKEN LIGHTLY

In 2011, I considered myself a veteran in regard to assessments. After all, I'd taken my fair share of them. My experience with completing assessments began while in college as an Army Reserve Officer Training Cadet (ROTC). During this training, we were required to conduct assessments on one another, and then we were professionally assessed for our individual occupation. I thought 360-degree assessments were detrimental, especially when one person did not like another. I later found out the assessment for our military occupation was also based on the needs of the military. (I did not get my first choice, and for my first four years, unbeknownst to my friends, peers, and leadership, I wanted to change my occupation.) We were not informed of the nuances of the assessment, and we did not question the process. I feared and dreaded an assessment and thought they were flawed and biased. Later in my career, while attending a leadership school, I obtained a greater understanding of assessments and realized their value and benefit.

In 2011, while sitting in Iraq, I received electronic notification of a 360-degree assessment that I was to complete on a fellow officer I had just met. My first thought was, *This is a joke.* I was not aware of his skills, knowledge, behavior, or competencies, and we had never worked together. I questioned why he would send me an assessment, and then it dawned on me: *He does not understand the tool.* I communicated with him that I could not fill out the assessment because I had only just met him. I do not remember all of his words, but I do remember he said, "Play along, and fill it out. It's anonymous." Regardless of his request, due to my understanding of the purpose and meaning of this tool, I did not complete it. Six months later, I continued to encourage him to consider the gravity of these tools and their proper use. I am still in disbelief that some have not grasped the purpose behind assessments and that they do not serve their intended use if administered improperly. It is not beneficial or useful if the assessment is simply sent to friends who will favorably comment or if the feedback received comes from those who are not familiar with the assessed individual or his or her performance. I hold to these beliefs. If someone I just met requests a 360-degree assessment from me, it is simply not going to happen!

TAKEAWAYS

Assessments are only as useful as the feedback discussion they initiate. It is important to prepare individuals for assessments and to receive feedback. Assessments are effective and efficient tools that provide feedback concerning preferences, abilities, skills, knowledge, experiences, competencies, behaviors, and styles of an individual. Within the assessment context, the feedback received occurs in a constructive and confidential manner. An assessment provides higher levels of self-awareness and insight for individuals to grow. Feedback offers another point of view, drives self-reflection, and reveals blind spots. Receiving wise counsel offers recipients with an understanding of how others view them and assists in adjusting both performances and behaviors.

CHAPTER 4
Similarities and Differences in
Mentoring and Coaching

Two are better than one, because they have a good reward for
their toil. For if they fall, one will lift up his fellow, but woe to him
who is alone when he falls and has not another to lift him up!
—Ecclesiastes 4:9–10 (ESV)

Once self-concept changes, behavior changes
to match the freshly perceived self.
—Carl Rogers

Experience: that most brutal of teachers. But
you learn, my God do you learn.
—C. S. Lewis

Mentoring and coaching both hold a significant role in
developing leaders. There are distinct differences between the
two, however, and their application is based on a core understanding
of these differences. In order to proceed effectively, both the
differences and the similarities between mentoring and coaching
must be clearly communicated to ensure correct application of these
two concepts and practices. Mislabeling can cause confusion, which
leads to a misunderstanding of concepts, processes, and procedures.
Regardless of which is used, however, it is of great importance
for leaders to weigh the cost when mentoring and coaching other
leaders. The value is not primarily monetary; it is a weighty cost in

terms of time, but it is worth the investment. Mentors and coaches are visionaries and often see past the current situation to move individuals to another place within the mentee or coachee.

There are hundreds of examples of coaching and mentoring in the Bible. When exploring deeper into mentoring and coaching, you will see there are notable similarities as well as differences between the two, and they are all important when faith-based leaders grow their leaders. Faith is the foundation of mentoring and coaching for both the coach and coachee; without it, development does not occur, according to the observations of Gary Collins, PhD, a licensed clinical psychologist and the author of over fifty books, including *Christian Coaching: Helping Others Turn Potential into Reality* (2009).

▌BIBLICAL MENTORING AND COACHING

Let me begin with key examples in the Bible of mentoring and coaching that are continuously relayed today, especially in Christendom. Many believers and Christian leaders are familiar with the great leaders in the Bible and how they understood and rose to a more significant position of power after first being selected by God. We often have been led to review and study their stories as case studies for our own development. The Bible teaches in Proverbs 12:15, "The way of the foolish is right in his own eyes, but a wise man listens to advice" (ESV). Learning is a result of a student, mentee, or coachee grasping concepts and applying them to his or her life, especially when wisdom is the cornerstone. Examples of godly understanding, counsel, and knowledge are plentiful in the Old Testament:

- Jethro mentored his son-in-law Moses (Exodus 18:13–27).
- Moses was a mentor and teacher for Joshua (Deuteronomy 3:28; 31:1–8).
- Naomi was a mentor, teacher, and coach for Ruth (the entire book of Ruth).

- Samuel was a mentor to Saul (1 Samuel 9:15-20)
- Samuel was a mentor to David (1 Samuel 16:10–13; 19:18).
- Jonathan was a mentor to David (1 Samuel 18:1–4; 19:1–7; and 20:1–42).
- Elijah was a mentor for Elisha (1 Kings 19:16–21; 2 Kings 1:1–16).

These mentoring and coaching relationships are just a sample of biblical examples from the Old Testament; they in no way exhaust the list.

When we explore the New Testament, there also are excellent and plentiful examples of mentoring and coaching.

- Elizabeth mentored and coached Mary (Luke 1: 36–56).
- Jesus was a mentor, teacher, and coach throughout the Gospels.
- Peter was a mentor and teacher to James, Cephas, and John (Galatians 2:7–14) and Silas (1 Peter 5:12–13).
- Ananias was a mentor to Saul (Acts 9:17–20).
- Barnabas was a mentor to Saul and the other apostles (Acts: 9:26–27; 11:25–26).
- Barnabas was a mentor to Mark, even after Paul's disagreement (Acts 15:37–39).
- Paul and Barnabas were mentors to Judas (Barabbas) and Silas.
- Paul was a mentor to Timothy, Luke, and Mark (2 Timothy 4:11).
- Paul was a mentor to Apollos (Acts18: 24–28).

This list of mentoring and coaching examples from the New Testament is also not exhaustive, but it shows how wise counsel catapults mentees or coachees.

It is vital for leaders to effectively understand the distinct differences between mentoring and coaching. Mentoring and coaching serve two distinct roles in development. Mentoring is teaching or telling others what to do and can be helpful in adopting a new method or behavior. The most critical element of mentoring is the bond or relationship that develops as a result of learning. Dr. Henry Talley (2008) believes mentoring is a creative way to promote professional development while assisting a process of growth and self-actualization. Mentoring pairs less experienced individuals with a more skilled and knowledgeable person who can be instrumental in professional development. Donna Augustine-Shaw (2015), believes mentoring demonstrates lessons from experiences and teaches best practices, which ultimately enforces shared visions when building leaders.

Coaching, however, is development. It assists with changing one's thinking regarding defined goals, objectives, and aspirations. It is a process of assisting others to release their potential to maximize their capacity and helping them in learning, which leads to results. Coaching an individual of faith involves deepening his or her call to serve and exploring with him or her how he or she plans to grow in concert with the Holy Spirit, all while focusing on the agenda of moving forward by asking questions to assist in gaining newer insights for newer actions.

The effects of coaching and mentoring do not cease when an individual mentor or coach is no longer around to administer sound words. The methods remain as part of a process that continues to grow. I have seen from personal experience in mentoring and coaching others that when leaders receive mentoring or coaching, they have a greater understanding of what they are called to do and are able to receive instruction more clearly from the Holy Spirit.

REFLECTION: KNOWING THE DIFFERENCE IN COACHING, TEACHING, AND MENTORING

The faith-based leaders in my life are a wealth of knowledge and are never apprehensive about sharing their love for the Lord and how important it is to ensure leaders in the church understand what it means to be a disciple. They demonstrate the availability to mentor, teach, and coach the members of the church and their leadership to where God has called them to be and do. The pastors under whom I serve (husband and wife team) have been key examples of mentoring and coaching that provided me with experiences. My pastor knew my passion for assisting others and began with coaching. The fact that the pastor has an understanding of the effectiveness of coaching and what it does was not a surprise because he also works with individuals who receive coaching services outside of the church. The pastor believes coaching involves communication with a coachee— who, when, what, how, and where will the goal be for them once achieved? He reminded me, that coaching is performance-driven; it is a process of how you grow and will dictate where you go.

When we reflected on mentoring, he reminded me mentoring involves developing for change as well as being available to and for the person. The pastor believes when an individual is living a life that demonstrates the fruits of the Spirit (Galatians 5:22) in all aspects of his/her daily life, he/she has a greater understanding of himself/ herself and can more easily make an adjustment, based on an outward demonstration of the mentor. The pastor believes teaching is conducted with words and action because instructions reveal, and education informs and assists in multiplying an individual's capacity. He thinks coaching is lacking in the church because leaders are required look at who needs what, and too often the senior leader does not have the time to do so. Instead of bringing an individual in to assist, the need continues to be unfilled.

Both of the pastors believe leadership in the church must consist of teaching, mentoring, and coaching. The pastors further think there is a need to grow, encourage, and stretch leaders in positions in the church. While increasing in influence, leaders need to ensure they (1) heard from God (the Holy Spirit), (2) remain teachable, and (3) understand the Holy Spirit regarding their calling. This can occur when the leader/coachee remains accountable through answering questions about how he or she is developing the gifts, talents, and calling in his or her life. When asked about their roles in others' lives, they said they are servants who desire to take care of others. They listen to an individual heart first, which leads them to be either a teacher or a mentor; if they cannot commit to a coaching relationship, they encourage coaching relationships with trusted leaders.

THE MENTOR

As mentioned above, mentoring takes on more of a teaching and instruction role in the life of the leader. The mentor and mentee must agree mentoring is not therapy. A mentor is a person who voluntarily teaches, supports, and encourages another person or group. A mentor provides a protégé with information, insights, and experiences (both good and bad) that have assisted or shaped the mentor into the modern man or woman. A mentor is a teacher, cheerleader, adviser, and counselor and is confident in his or her skills, abilities, and knowledge. A mentor is a good listener who communicates well and ensures the protégé that their conversations are between the two of them (unless he or she intends to harm himself/herself or others). Mentors are highly valuable, especially in religious organizations. There is minimal to no monetary obligation, and, if conducted in a meaningful manner, such a relationship causes mind-set shifts and assists individuals to look at a situation three-dimensionally. Andrew Satter and Diane Russ (2007) believe there are benefits in mentoring between more senior leaders and younger executives. The belief is there is an increased effectiveness and motivation of emerging leaders when mentoring is involved; it also lowers organizational turnover rates of the next generation of leaders because it develops, engages, and prepares an individual for the next level of responsibilities. The principle of mentoring is also useful in the church. From biblical history, it has proven to be effective and has long-lasting effects. Mentors do not focus on skills improvement; the interest is in developing.

Many faith-based leaders have come to recognize that formal mentoring may not be a part of the church's culture. This does not mean it has to remain this way. Mentoring does have a cost, but that is time. Many leaders will attest that they do not have time to mentor others, so the question that needs to be answered is, if you do not have time to mentor your leaders, where are they receiving counsel? Any counsel will not fit, especially for leaders in the church; the Bible provides everything you need for delivering counsel. First Timothy 3:16–17 teaches "all scripture is breathed out by God, and profitable for training, reproof, for correction, and for training righteousness, that the man of God may be complete, equipped for every good work" (ESV).

Mentoring and teaching provide guidance, advice, and recommendations; mentoring assists in solving problems by providing a tried method that leads to success. Proverbs 9:9 says, "Give instruction to a wise man, and he will be wiser; teach a righteous man, and he will increase in learning" (ESV). Mentoring is not making others a carbon copy of who you are but rather telling others how to become successful. Mentoring is either formal or informal. Formal mentors are either assigned for development purposes or formed through friendship or because of a close relationship. A mentoring relationship is effective and received when it is not forced upon an individual group. Mentoring requires shared values and commitment; without the two, the relationship will not work.

COACHING

An excellent coach is hard to find, difficult to
part with and impossible to forget.
—unknown

A coach is not a therapist. A coach does not tell an individual what he or she needs to do. A coach's focus is on actions. A coach is not an expert in every possible prospective field of interest, nor does he need to be. The International Coach Federation (ICF) (n.d.) "defines coaching as partnering with clients in a thought-provoking and creative process that inspires them to maximize their personal and professional potential" ("Core Competencies," n.d.).

ICF identifies the core competencies of coaching as follows: (1) Establish a foundation; this includes adhering to ethical guidelines and professional standard. (2) Co-create a relationship with a coachee through building trust and being present. (3) Communicate effectively through active listening and asking thought-provoking questions. (4) Facilitate learning and results through awareness, actions, planning, and goal setting by managing progress, and hold the coachee accountable for doing what he or she says he/she will do.

Christian coaching is what Tony Stoltzfus (2013) describes as living toward heaven while aligning our lives to maximize the eternal payoff. Stoltzfus also believes Christian coaching assists believers in discovering the unique calls on their lives and how to manage them. Christian coaching assists believers to give through serving according to God's way and will. Christian coaching assists coachees to find possible means to live in preparation for eternal reward. Christian coaching involves assisting a coachee to discover the role of a representative of Christ by the works he or she does for the kingdom. First Timothy 4:12, 14–15 says, "Do not neglect the gift you have, which was given you by prophecy when the council of elders laid their hands on you. Practice these things, immerse yourself in them, so that all may see your progress" (ESV).

Coaching is a process of assisting others to release their potential to maximize their capacity, and it helps them in learning, which leads to results from a growth mind-set. Coaching requires reflection of what occurred, including what was done to affect the outcome, what were practical strategies, and what were the lessons learned. Coaching facilitates more in-depth learning, strategizing, and appreciative works; it involves risk-taking and working toward better results because of the possibilities that exist. Coaching is not a command in the Bible, and there are no directives. When we consider what we are supposed to do, however, such as encouraging, having an ear to hear what the Holy Spirit is saying, and doing what God calls us to do, coaching entails all of these. In chapter 1, the definition and concept of coaching were discussed as a reminder that essential coaching requires listening and asking questions that focus on the coachee's performance and development, which leads to change and growth. The most critical skill in coaching is listening! Not every person knows how to listen well, and listening is a crucial skill in a coaching relationship. Listening to a coachee requires watching both verbal and nonverbal cues. This leads to the root cause and is also essential in developing and asking thought-provoking questions.

CHRISTIAN COACHING

As a Christian, it is essential to discuss the importance of Christian coaching because of the significance of the Holy Spirit guiding the coach and coachee. There are Christian coaching organizations that align their professional standards for the coach with the International Coach Federation (ICF) and understand the powerful influence coaching has on coachees through awareness and assisting a coachee to move toward his or her goals. Faith-based leaders must also be careful to keep in mind professional Christian life coaches differ in their approaches to coaching than secular coaches. Christianlifecoaching.com has an interesting take on how Christian life coaching differs; they believe a coach serves the role of a detective. Detectives do not know the answers; they ask profound questions for the sake of obtaining an awareness and growth.

Coaching in faith-based settings is not as accepted as in mainstream culture because many churches and leaders are apprehensive that coaching might interfere with values and virtues. Dr. Gary Collins (2009) concludes the demonstrated cultural insensitivity of a coach might explain why some groups reject coaching and miss the importance and benefits that coaching brings. He also believes faith-based leaders are influenced by the experiences of others and can best be introduced to coaching from those who have experienced it. By observing and hearing about the success coaching has on others (either other church members or leaders from other faith-based organizations), they can be introduced to the initiatives of faith-based coaching programs. Proverbs 20:5

reminds believers, "The purpose in a man's heart is like deep water, but a man of understanding will draw it out" (ESV).

Another pioneer who has been influential in bringing the coaching profession to faith-based organizations is Tony Stoltzfus. Stoltzfus (2005) confers the difficulty many coaches have is in refraining from telling coachees what to do or providing advice. The initial challenge many Christian coaches face is a result of their position to serve others from what is in their hearts. Stoltzfus believes, "When you begin to think like a coach, believe in the coaching values and see others through the eyes of a coach, the coaching skills come naturally" (2). The heart of a Christian coach does not listen primarily because of the core skills of coaching; he or she listens to the coachee because coaching is practicing the discipline of believing in people to empower them to change.

OLD AND NEW TESTAMENT COACHING AND MENTORING

A coach helps the coachee develop a vision. He or she asks thought-provoking questions to assist the coachee in exploring other possibilities. When we look for examples of coaching in the New Testament, Paul, Barnabas, and Jesus are prime examples of who, in modern day, would be called executive or master coaches. Paul's instruction for coaching is visible in Ephesians 4:11–13:

> And he gave the apostles, the prophets, the evangelists, the shepherds and teachers, to equip the saints for the work of ministry, for building up the body of Christ, until we all attain to the unity of the faith and of the knowledge of the Son of God, to mature manhood, to the measure of the stature of the fullness of Christ. (ESV)

Paul reveals the structure of the church and how it grows, which depends solely on Christ. Paul's description of the structure and how to live through Christ is the standard. His writings tell us how each person called into position is to work (through prayer and hearing from the Holy Spirit). Paul further reminds believers they will know that what they are doing is according to their calling because of the peace that will present itself. Paul helps readers understand how to stay in touch with cultural shifting, and he spoke in a manner that allowed others to know he did not falter in his beliefs. Paul was aware of what was occurring at the time and, as a result, encouraged, assisted, and equipped others for the work of spreading the gospel.

Psalm 23 presents a poignant example of God as the first and master executive and still-reigning coach. In this psalm, David recognized his calling and who keeps him, who encourages him, and who walks alongside him. David remembered his experience as a shepherd and that he knew his sheep, and they knew his voice. Just as with David, I appeal to you as a faith-based leader to consider this truth: The Father God personally coaches you. He knows you by your name and your calling. In turn, leaders within your organization follow and look to you to provide provision (teaching), guidance, and protection. As you appoint leaders to serve with you, ask questions of them to ensure they are following the moral compass, which is Christ.

The senior leader in a faith-based organization must know his or her leaders are not weak and are obedient in observing how the Holy Spirit leads. Followers and leaders alike within your organization should seek to please the Lord, not you as a leader. Christian coaching initiatives follow the Holy Spirit and focus on pleasing God alone. Faith-based leaders provide a safe place for other leaders to plan, while keeping the truths of Jeremiah 29:11 in mind. Jesus reminds believers in John 14:26 that the Holy Spirit is a teacher and guide. The coachee is better equipped to lead others because the plan is directed by the Holy Spirit, is carefully considered, and has an expected outcome that is pleasing to and serves Christ.

▌TAKEAWAYS

Although there is no specified command to mentor or coach in the Bible, there are many mandates and exhortations that align with core coaching and mentoring precepts. Leaders follow this biblical standard when, through experience and wisdom, they assist others to reach a higher level of success by applying creative and innovative ways to accomplish their missions. Mentoring and coaching serve separate purposes throughout the Bible, and both require attentive listening. Both teaching and mentoring provide a leader who helps the individual grow and develop. A mentor shares experience, discusses best practices, and provides instruction and advice for needed growth. A coach focuses on active listening, asking powerful questions, developing a vision for change, and providing accountability for attainment of goals.

CHAPTER 5
Leadership That Affects Coaching

So, God created man in his own image, in the image of
God he created him; male and female he created them. And
God blessed them. And God said to them, "Be fruitful and
multiply and fill the earth and subdue it, and have dominion
over the fish of the sea, and over the birds of the heavens
and over every living thing that moves on the earth."
—Genesis: 1:27–28 (ESV)

The first job in leadership is to love people.
Leadership without love is manipulation.
—Rick Warren

When pondering leadership as a Christian, one must start with
the beginning of time. God, the ultimate leader, created
man in His image and commanded him to "be fruitful and multiply
and fill the earth ..." (ESV). As we look at leadership that affects
coaching, being fruitful and multiplying calls for encouraging,
caring, valuing, and assisting others to become productive in what
they are gifted, according to God's will for their lives. The tangible
effects of coaching in organizations begin with leadership. According
to James Autry (2004), the author of *Servant Leadership: How to Build
a Creative Team, Develop Great Morale, and Improve Bottom-Line
Performance*, real leadership is not merely a compilation of theories,
behaviors, and styles; instead, it is in keeping with the premise
that what you do as a leader solely depends on who you are. The

leadership theories and styles explained in this chapter define how daily organizational operations (whether faith-based or corporate) are affected by beliefs, practices, and procedures that have been around for many years. Thousands of books, seminars, websites, and motivational speakers claim to have the answer for what is the best leadership theory or style, due to changes in world events or cultural shifts. As a leader in any organization, there are many competing answers regarding which leadership style best suits your organization. What determines the right one is conditional and contingent? The list of leadership styles most comparable to coaching is more exhaustive than what will be covered in this chapter. Representative sampling, however, is provided and detailed to provide a foundation for such a comparison. It is important as leaders to remember there are many leadership theories, styles, characteristics, and behaviors that affect coaching. Leaders will benefit from understanding approaches that are instrumental in coaching, such as path-goal and leader-member exchange and how a shift occurs in behaviors and relationships. It is essential to understand how the behaviors displayed by leaders affect coaching through their reflection of directive, supportive, participative, or achievement-oriented roles. There are many leadership styles; those that are most conducive to coaching are transformational, charismatic, servant, and Christian leadership.

Before taking an exploration of sample leadership theories and styles, let's take another look at leadership. Leadership is the ability to influence others. Leaders also know their own knowledge, power, management abilities, and strengths. Leadership provides direction, strategy, and purpose. Peter Northouse defines leadership as "a process whereby an individual influence a group of individuals to achieve a common goal" (5). In Charles W. Naylor's (1982) book *Heart Talks*, he believes "man is capable of great development" (84), and the blessing from God over man's life will aid in one's endeavors, but we have to be unwavering and preserve efforts. This means leaders who are called to do the work of God must have a desire to be successful, and before we can do the job for God conclusively, we must know ourselves.

The elephant in the room lends these questions:

1. What leadership theory and style do you have as a leader?
2. When was your last leadership assessment?
3. Have you adjusted over the previous five years (why or why not)?

I pause to ask these questions because possessing a healthy sense of one's leadership theory approach and style is crucial when working with others, regardless of the organizational context. Naylor further reminds us of the apostle Paul's conversation with his disciple Timothy. "Neglect not the gift that is in thee ..." (1 Timothy 4:14 ESV). Several leadership theories and types significantly affect coaching. It is important to know which type of leader you are and which styles you employ.

This chapter presents a more in-depth exploration of leadership theories and styles that are instrumental outside the church and adopted within the church, with the Word of God encasing the methods. In this chapter, I will introduce several leadership styles, such as Nehemiah's excellent leadership model from the Old Testament. The two critical edifices Nehemiah was charged to rebuild were a physical wall and the edifice of faith-based lives. Nehemiah's leadership example demonstrates how the power of God is the most important theory and style when coaching others. Proverbs 16:7 is also a reminder: "When a man's ways please the Lord, he makes even his enemies to be at peace with him" (ESV). I will discuss various types of behaviors: directive, supportive, participative, and achievement-oriented. I will also discuss theories such as path-goal and leader-member theories, as well as transformational and charismatic, servant, and Christian leadership models and their effects on coaching.

Faith-based leaders, especially Christians, believe God looks at the heart of the leader, not merely his or her theory or style. When leaders follow the Holy Spirit, mistakes are minimal. This does not mean one has to be perfect, but when applying wisdom to what you do, as a leader, errors are reduced because of sound faith-based advice. Some faith-based leaders follow a secular way of leading. Not wanting to risk offending called lay leaders, some bend and bring the theories and styles of business leadership practices into their organizations. Although there is nothing wrong with adopting business theories and methods, they must not interfere with the values and doctrines of Christ, and the leader should continue to listen primarily to the Holy Spirit. God has every desire for men and women to develop, build, and rebuild the body of believers and the leader. It is vital for faith-based leaders to know which leadership theory or style governs their way of thinking and behavior. A specific leadership style or theory does not impress God; instead, what God desires of any leader are integrity, love, and abiding by the Holy Spirit. It does not matter what your leadership style is; remember, you will face challenges. You have to win trust. Leaders must be authentic, earn respect, and remain curious, especially while coaching others.

LEADERSHIP THEORIES

Why are leadership theories so critical, especially when it comes to leaders and coaching? As leaders, it is crucial to look for answers that are practical, applicable, and as easy to remember as truth when it comes to coaching others. Peter elicits this core understanding within listeners when he reminds the leaders who are shepherding God's people:

> Shepherd the flock of God that is among you, exercising oversight, not under compulsion, but willingly, as God would have you; not for shameful gain, but eagerly; not domineering over those in your charge, but being examples to the flock. (1 Peter 5:2–3 ESV)

When applying leadership theories in coaching, it is important also to be the example. The expectation is to develop leadership skills within your coachee. Peter identified with the elders in 1 Peter 5:2–3, which allowed him to listen to them and not tell them what to do. Peter's leadership training, theory, and style came from Jesus. Leadership theories are what you believe and value. In faith-based organizations, the faith-based leader usually sets the tone of operating theory based on cross-cultural nuances.

PATH-GOAL THEORY

The path-goal theory primarily affects how a leader motivates others to accomplish goals. Path-goal theory is useful with coaching because the leaders (coaches) look for ways to enhance the coachee's performance by focusing on the motivation behind the goal. In other words, the path-goal theory is a derivative of expectancy theory. When the leader (coach) selects the correct path-goal style, he or she allows the coachee to maneuver the charted course to achieve his or her goal. Path-goal requires one question that causes the coachee to move according to the goal he/she has set. Keith Webb (2015), author of *Coaching in Ministry: How Busy Church Leaders Can Multiply Their Ministry Impact*, asks, "What actions could you take to move forward?" (72). Path-goal theory is useful in coaching leaders in faith-based organizations because it keeps the coachee working toward hearing from the Holy Spirit and asking questions related to what the next change might look like for himself/herself and his/her ministry. Other questions one might ask:

1. Where will this lead the ministry and me?
2. How will I accomplish this for the sake of the ministry?
3. Why is it important, and where is the Holy Spirit leading me to the ministry?

Path-goal causes the leader (coach) to shift behaviors that are directive, supportive, participative, and achievement-oriented when interacting with the coachee.

▌LEADER-MEMBER EXCHANGE THEORY

Leader-member exchange (LMX) theory is a dyadic relationship between the leader and follower. Katrina Lloyd, Diana Boer, and Sven Voelpel (2017) denote the LMX theory, at its core, suggests "effective leadership processes occur when leaders and followers can develop a mature leadership relationship" (432). The leader and the follower listen in a nonjudgmental manner to achieve a goal. The follower is willing to participate in a way that goes beyond the ordinary duty description. Faith-based leaders who understand how effective LMX is with coaching are likely to have better communication with the lay leader (coachee). There are tangible commitments and actions, as well as performance improvement, to help in achieving goals because of the communication flow between the leader and follower.

▌BEHAVIOR-LEADER THEORY

Behaviors govern how leaders engage and communicate with followers. In faith-based organizations, the leader's behavior has an enormous effect on the coaching relationships and his or her ability to coach objectively. Erica Anthony (2017), author of *The Impact of Leadership Coaching on Leadership Behaviors*, suggests, "Leaders who seek to develop followers will also demonstrate delegating behaviors" (932). Anthony also believes faith-based leaders with positive coaching experiences are more likely to match the positive behavior and values when coaching others; this is an example of learned reaction or response to a decisive action. Behaviors in coaching are directive, supportive, participative, and achievement-oriented. Directive behavior causes the leader (coach) to give assignments to the coachee. This also holds the coachee responsible for his or her actions.

Nehemiah was a leader whose directive behavior was instrumental in the people of Jerusalem building the wall. Peter Northouse defines directive behavior in the initial coaching engagements as that which provides the coachee with clarification of what he or she is responsible for, how often it will occur, and how it will happen (in writing or oral reports of progress). Leaders who are directive when coaching their leaders empower the coachees to take charge of the coaching sessions. This frees the coach to ask questions, observe, and adjust the former or demonstrated performance in decision making.

Supportive behavior-leader coaches are listeners who involve communication and response. This includes asking for input regarding how he or she will solve the problem. Supportive leaders go out of their way to make the environment pleasant, which is a vital element in coaching. Coaching is intended to be safe and judgment-free. Supportive behaviors of a leader coach include praising the coachee, sharing information about self without crossing into mentoring, and listening. Supportive behaviors also involve loyalty and faithfulness through being present for coaching engagements, committing to assisting the coachee, being flexible, and being supportive of growth and development. Supportive leadership behavior does not tell; it encourages and guides. Leader coaches must be supportive of decisions made by coachees and allow them to see where an adjustment is needed through trial and error. Leader coaches must remember the coachee also hears from the Holy Spirit regarding how, what, when, and where to move from the current place to a higher one.

Participative leadership behavior is not an integral part of coaching for the leader as much as it is for the coachee. The leader coach does not elicit from the coachee; instead, the leader coach asks the coachee thought-provoking questions, driving how he or she makes decisions. The achievement-oriented leadership behavior challenges followers and coachees to do their best. A leader whose coaching behavior is achievement-oriented sets challenging goals for the coachee and has faith in the coachee's abilities. The faith-based leader coach expects the coachee to perform at a higher level than usual because of the confidence he or she has in the lay leader's ability. The leader coach then operates in many leadership behaviors and styles; this is considered as situational leadership. Peter

Northouse (2013) suggests leaders should adapt their style to the situation or the motivational need of an individual.

▌LEADERSHIP STYLES

In an article titled, "Leadership Styles of Prominent Figures in the Bible," Joyce Bott, provides an explanation of various modern-day leadership styles from a biblical perspective and further explains how these leadership styles can have an effect when coaching. God's leadership style appears as transactional. Faith-based leaders who are transactional are more mentors and teachers, rather than coaches, when they step in when there is a problem. Moses was a transformational leader. Faith-based leaders who are transformational leaders help the coachees reach their goals by asking questions and assisting them in adjusting how they think and react, thus causing a shift in previously learned behaviors that affect performances. Transformational leaders change by moving coachees from their current status by reminding them of their purpose, goal, and vision.

Saul was a charismatic leader. He personified strength and was handsome and fearless. Faith-based leaders who employ the charismatic leadership style in coaching will enable the coachee to believe he or she is capable of achieving goals because the charismatic leader (coach) can communicate hope. In *Being Leaders: The Nature of Authentic Christian Leadership*, author Aubrey Malphurs (2003) asks, "Is a Christian leader only a leader in a Christian context or is he a Christian leader in all contexts?" (13). The answer to the question is that a Christian leader is the same inside and outside because of the conversion experience. Scripture reminds believers, "Therefore, if anyone is in Christ, he is a new creation. The old has passed away; behold, the new has come" (2 Corinthians 5:17). Christian leadership is not a style but a way of life.

Visionary, directional, strategic, managing, motivating, shepherding, team-building, entrepreneurial, reengineering, and bridge-building are all effective leadership styles when motivating followers. Each of these styles has its place in traditional leadership styles, such as transformational (or, as some prefer, charismatic), while servant, authentic, and transactional leadership have been around for many years. Articles and studies have shown that transformational or charismatic leadership was the type of leadership Jesus demonstrated while on earth. Leadership styles are merely methods; as a leader, it is essential not to center oneself on a style by remembering that the Holy Spirit will lead the style of leadership He desires for you because of the situations and circumstances you experience.

▌SERVANT LEADERSHIP

Servant leadership is a calling, an awareness, a stewardship, listening, persuasion, growth, empathy, foresight, community building, healing, and conceptualization. Peter Northouse (2013) repeats the notion that "servant leaders put followers first, empower them, and help them develop their full personal capacities" (219). Another definition of servant leadership fitting for coaching is the belief of David Kuhnert (2016), the author of *Servant Leadership: Influencing Others to Get There by Leading a Transformational Life*: It is "influencing others to get there" (5). The path taken for an individual to get from here to there is filled with action, learning, and adjusting. Paul provides a reminder in Philippians 2:3–4: "Do nothing from selfish ambition or conceit but in humility count others more significant than yourself. Let each of you look not only to his interests but also to the interests of others" (ESV).

Coaches who are servant leaders in faith-based organizations understand it will take work and faith for the coachee to reach his or her goal. The servant-leader coach is instrumental in asking thought-provoking questions that motivate the coachee in developing a course of action. The servant-leader coach empowers the coachee through the process of identifying the purpose of the goal. The leader then assists the coachee to move from the *why* to make the goal relevant, realistic, and attainable. Servant leaders can help coachees understand the complexities of individuals or situations and then can assist them in working through issues. Servant leaders are empathic to the needs of the persons they serve.

CHRISTIAN LEADERSHIP

Christian leaders differ from leaders in general because they live as believers who have accepted Christ as their personal Savior. Christian leaders are under submission and are moral leaders who also have a personal relationship with God. Author Aubrey Malphurs (2003) further asserts "they must put themselves under the lordship of Christ" (15). Their source comes from hearing from the Holy Spirit. Christian leaders are essential when coaching others because they are there to serve the coachee and not their own agenda. Proverbs 11:14 says, "Where there is no guidance, a people fall, but in an abundance of counselors there is safety" (ESV). As the shepherd, pastor, and head of the church, faith-based leaders in faith-based organizations must understand that the leaders who serve under them are there to assist in hearing from God what they are called to do and to help in kingdom building.

TAKEAWAYS

Numerous emerging leadership styles are studied and profiled in the modern age. It is interesting to read newfound theories and styles with enormous undertones of historical methods. The theories and styles mentioned throughout this chapter do not exhaust the list of theories and styles. However, years of tested, tried, and successful theories (such as goal-path and leader-member exchange) and leadership styles (such as transformational/charismatic, servant, and Christian leadership) have proven effective for leaders who identify with them. These theories and styles are not the only valid theories but are referred to as an example of leaders' beliefs that affect leadership methods. The methods, theories, and styles mentioned in this chapter are mere suggestions. The most important takeaway is first to understand what type of leader you are, as well as the model of leadership you are providing in your coaching services. Ensure your methods, theory, and style are based on the situation at hand, and be prepared to shift as the Holy Spirit leads. As a Christian coach, you must still follow the agenda of the client/coachee. The competencies and standards of coaching and the service to the individual is not a one-size-fits-all. It is important to know other leadership theories, styles, and methods while assisting others to reach their goals.

When you, as the faith-based leader coach, sit down to assess a coachee, ask him or her what vision he or she has for the church. The faith-based leaders should ask how they fit in and then ask what their vision is. Asking this question may change which leadership style you adopt while coaching the coachee. Remember that the methods you use as a leader coach will depend on the situation. Keep in mind that even if you think you know your leadership theory, style, and behavior, and you have been operating as such for years (even with a level of success), do not be surprised when it changes. Faith-based Christian leaders know God has a way of changing how they live their lives.

Saul in the New Testament is one of the best examples of such change. The Holy Spirit lives in Christians' hearts and governs their actions. When leaders are called into leadership positions, they must remain submissive to God. A leadership style, theory, or behavior is not set in stone. The transformational/charismatic or servant-leadership style is subject to change, depending on the situation. Christian leaders must not fixate on one leadership style to be effective as a leader and a coach.

CHAPTER 6
The Characteristics and Competencies of a Leader or Coach Matter

People do not care how much you know until
they know how much you care.
—Teddy Roosevelt

But the fruit of the Spirit is love, joy, peace, patience,
kindness, goodness, faithfulness, gentleness, self-
control; against such things, there is no law.
—Galatians 5:22–23 (ESV)

Your character is who you are; your competencies are learned and acquired formally or informally. I state this because of what I have experienced, learned, and observed, based on my rearing from childhood, as a college student, as an officer/leader in the military, and as a leader in the church. People trust you when are constant, honest, dependable, caring, and, most of all, loyal. People know when you genuinely care for them, and then they are interested in what you know and how you can assist them in their time of need. Since not every leader considers himself or herself a servant leader, this chapter focuses on the core competencies and characteristics of leadership, regardless of one's leadership style. In this chapter, I will discuss the characteristics and skills of a leader or coach and why both matters. Remember, coaching requires creating a safe environment to discuss intimate details of plans and goals that are judgment-free.

As a Christian coach, displaying the fruit of the Spirit changes one's character to reflect that of Christ. The fruit of the Spirit is a chain reaction of traits and characteristics, meaning each lead into the other and are manifested as one, just as Jesus. As a Christian leader, not operating in the fruit of the Spirit handicaps oneself as well as others. How much longer will we, as leaders, continue to allow this to happen in our organizations? In some of the churches in which I have served as a leader, heated discussions have caused many to question the abilities of selected leaders due to indiscretions from the past. Why do I cite Galatians 5:22–23 as a core mantra for leadership? This particular passage speaks to the character of an individual.

Walking and living in the fruit of the Spirit is not living as an à la carte, where you select which characteristics you desire; you must possess all of them. A Bible study on Christian character led me to purchase nine separate books about the fruit of the Spirit. Each book provides knowledge that gives clarity and understanding of the Christlike characteristics that should govern your life. I remember a pastor saying the fruit of the Spirit is not an option, especially when you lead others. Aubrey Malphurs (2003), author of *Being Leaders: The Nature of Authentic Christian Leadership*, provides readers with a valuable takeaway: When Christ is in a believer, others will see what is also in Christ.

Why discuss character and competencies in regard to coaching? As a leader, your character speaks for you in your absence—it is your reputation. Christian leaders understand there is an expectation of being free of controversy; if and when controversy precedes you, there will be a great deal of consternation in tow. While researching and reading what to discuss regarding character, a pastor of a local church reminded me of Timothy and the instructions he provided regarding the individual character of leaders in the church. A leader in the church must be beyond reproach. This statement may appear to be a utopian thought and perhaps unattainable today, but for a leader, it is crucial. Quite a few Christians desire a leader who encompasses godly character, such as is found in the life of Nehemiah. I recall encounters from experience and serving in leadership positions since the early 1990s. The character of a person is and has been an essential aspect of leadership and makes a profound difference. Without it, there is constant questioning, doubt, and frustrations that can lead to chaos.

How much longer must we experience a questioned character of an individual in a leadership position, faith-based or non–faith-based? An individual's character and competencies are not considered a legal matter and are not subject to a statute of limitations. There is no rule to say, after a specific time, one is void of being upright and accountable. The character of a person should speak in his or her absence. Competency, on the other hand, changes with time, education, and experience. The character of a leader (or any person) cannot be placed to the side and picked up as needed, depending on the situation.

As a leader in the world of business and the church, I view one's character as similar to deoxyribonucleic acid (DNA). Scientists define DNA as a molecule that carries the genetic instructions used in the growth, development, functioning, and reproduction of all known living organisms and many viruses. I also view character as who you are, and when there is a question about an action, someone will defend your honor and say, "This is out of character and hard for me to believe about you." An individual's character grows, develops, and functions and is strengthened through experiences that cause him or her to do what is considered as usual for the individual.

It is hard to face the heartbreak, disappointment, and shock many experiences when hearing of accusations regarding the character of a leader, whether in positions of authority in local, state, or federal government or in religious organizations. In such scenarios, the character of a person is debatable, and there are discussions as to what is considered reasonable or rational. The other side of the argument believes when a person behaves out of the norm of character, it does not take away from his or her competencies or the anointing that is on that person. Coaching, just like character, is not new, yet many are still new to how effective it is and how it moves individuals—primarily leaders—who are serious about a change from being stuck in their current state. When referring to coaching, competencies, and characteristics (or as I call them, the 3 C's), there is an alignment of the attributes of the three that lean toward servant leadership. The characteristics/attributes of servant leadership and the core competencies of coaching are designed to partner with each other to inspire individuals to reach their maximum potential, professionally and on a personal basis (or, in a religious setting, one's calling).

In chapter 5, several leadership theories were discussed. Now we will look at several characteristics of a leader. There is a difference between competencies and character. Galatians 5:22–23 is an identifiable and favored text of many Christian leaders when discussing character and how leaders should live their lives, as supported by 1 Timothy 3. The fruit of the Spirit is who you are, no matter what. These attributes are in your being as a person, whether you operate in sacred or secular settings. The sacred texts teach us the fruit of the Spirit comes from the Holy Spirit, which are character traits that are also like Jesus the Christ, as mentioned earlier. These characteristics are automatic once you give your life to Christ, but they are developed through the new creation each believer becomes as he or she is discipled and strengthened in the faith. The discipline occurs through connecting with Jesus, as described in John 15:4–5:

> Abide in me, and I in you. As the branch cannot bear
> fruit by itself, unless it abides in the vine, neither can
> you, unless you abide in me. I am the vine; you are
> the branches. Whoever abides in me and I in him,
> he it is that bears much fruit, for apart from me you
> can do nothing. (ESV)

John 15:4–5 teaches the importance of abiding in Christ, the provider of nourishment for growth and development in an individual. When one does not correctly receive sources to aid in growing, he or she dies. The fruit of the Spirit changes the former ingrained ways and causes newer action and reaction toward circumstances in situations. Paul is a prime example of a genuine transformation of one's character after his Damascus experience. Paul formerly persecuted others, but the Holy Spirit questioned him: "And falling to the ground, he heard a voice saying to him, 'Saul, Saul, why are you persecuting me?'" (Acts 9:4 ESV).

WHY ARE CHARACTER AND COMPETENCIES IMPORTANT?

There are scores of written and oral seminars and lectures on the importance of an individual's character, competencies, and skills. James Hunter (2004), author of *The Most Powerful Leadership Principle: How to Become a Servant Leader*, believes one's character is what a man (or woman) is when in the dark; one's character is similar to a moving target that continues to develop and grow in life. Hunter further offers the notion that character is encompassed by habits that encapsulate an individual's vices and virtue. Hunter reminds readers of an ancient statement: "Thoughts become actions, actions become habits, habits become our character, and our character may determine our destiny" (147), but one's character is not determined by destiny. Your character will take you where your skills, talents, and competencies cannot because it is defined by who you are when you are alone and when nobody is watching.

I am pausing here to make a few clarifications for character and its characteristics, competencies, and skills. The word *character* is a noun that describes what is typical of an individual, place, or thing. The characteristics and competencies of any person are essential when leading others. It does not matter how many degrees you hold, how affluent you are, or how many awards you have for your works if you fail to walk in character. Understanding your leadership style and what theory model you align with is essential, but technique and theory can change because of character change, development, competencies, learning skills, and attributes. The questions I often ask leaders are, why does character or competency matter, and why should leaders care about doing better in any organization, whether faith-based or secular? This comes from a desire to understand how some respond to 2 Corinthians 8:7: "But as you excel in everything—in faith, in speech, in knowledge, and in all eagerness and in love from us that is in you—make sure that you excel in this act of kindness too" (ESV).

The author of *The Making of a Christian Leader*, Ted Engstrom (1976), believes one's character is what some refer to as your "credit rating" (113); it includes but not limited to honesty, consistency, loyalty, ethics, and morals. Engstrom also believed the more character and competency others see in you, the more confident they are with what you say, request, or suggest. I have a sincere appreciation for the thoughtful words of Andy Stanley (2003), author of *The Next Generation Leader*, who recommends you upgrade your current performance through your strengths and delegate areas in which you are not as strong. In doing so, you will enhance productivity and focus.

REFLECTION: REMAIN APPROACHABLE

In the late 1990s, as a captain in the US Army, I was stationed in Panama. A fellow officer, Barren (not his real name), reminded me to remain approachable, no matter what. I asked Barren to explain what he meant by that. He told me I always appeared focused, with squinted eyes, but once we partnered in class, he changed his opinion. He saw me as others had told him I was: focused, yet a selfless leader who loved to advance others; a friend. Barren said, "Your physical characteristics throw others off, and they are not sure if you will be receptive to them." A couple of weeks after the class ended, I saw him again and asked for greater clarification, revealing that an eye injury caused me to squint in bright sunlight, and vanity kept me from wearing glasses. Barren suggested I consider purchasing prescription glasses with a tint to wear when in the sun. He believed it would change my physical characteristics. He said the characteristics I possessed and wished to portray—a caring and giving friend, great listener, sensitive to the needs of others, putting others first all the time, meek, faithful, fair, stern, and loving as an energetic leader in the church and on the job—would be seen in another light. Barren thought others would gravitate to those things instead of being turned off by my frown and stern look. Barren also reminded me that being a leader who cares is more valuable than a leader who does not.

Barren's statements caused me to rethink how some things are ingrained, and some things can be changed. Since the late '90s, I have taken his practical advice to help others see this side of me. His comments caused what I later learned was a mind-set shift that affected not only my perceived image but also my actions. After leaving Panama, a young lady came up to me at Fort Bragg and said, "I remember you from Panama. Do you have a minute?" Although I did not have it, I made time because she needed someone to listen to her and be there for her. This was a reflection of the change that had taken place. Years later, I ran into Barren and was able to share with him how his advice had paid off. I thanked him and reminded him of our conversations while in Panama and how his comments had shaped me as a leader and caused me to *remain approachable*!

COMPETENCIES AND CHARACTERISTICS OF LEADERSHIP

Andy Stanley (2003) believed it is important for leaders to direct their energies toward areas in which they will excel because of experience and knowledge and to remember, as a leader, that character is what ignites others to follow. The challenges leaders face are centered on two things: competencies and character, which affect everything they say or do when it comes to people. What are the differences in competencies and character? Typically, competencies are unpredictable yet expected behaviors and skills, while character is learned behavior because of experiences and learning. Why does competency matter? Should leaders care about doing well? Leaders in faith-based and non–faith-based organizations alike are expected to demonstrate certain traits, such as empowering others, moral standards and judgment, intelligence, interpersonal skills, prudence, courage, decision-making abilities, influence, and fairness. This is by no means an exhaustive list, but it does give an indication of what can be expected of leaders in various contexts. Sunnie Giles (2016), a contributing writer for *Harvard Business Review,* and Ronald D. Riggio, PhD (2014), contributing writer for *Psychology Today,* believe leadership competencies are both challenging and often difficult, and leaders must understand they cannot do everything alone; rather, it takes followers who are willing to assist in accomplishing the expected competencies.

CHARACTERISTICS OF A SERVANT LEADER

It is important to remember, as a leader, that others have a higher expectation of your character and competencies. A leader who has openly questionable character flaws and does not appear competent is often looked upon as untrustworthy or is not considered as a servant leader because some actions are more selfish than a selfless act for the good of others. N. T. Wright (2010) begins *After You Believe: Why Christian Character Matters* with a conversation he had with a young man who had an encounter that awakened his understanding of who God is. The young man was having a difficult time with what others told him and what the Bible teaches about God's unconditional love—accepting you for who you are—while on the other end of the spectrum, there is an expectation to share the gospel and live a life confined by rules that have the ability to debilitate and stifle. Wright explained character is transforming: "Character-, the transforming, shaping and marking of a life and its habits- will generate the sort of behavior that rules might have pointed toward but which a "rule-keeping" mentality can never achieve". (7)

It bears repeating that a servant leader is one who is a servant first. Servant leaders are selfless in many ways because they desire to bring others to a higher place in various areas of their lives for the sake of wholeness. Daniel Harkvay (2007), author of *Becoming a*

Coaching Leader: The Proven Strategy for Building Your Own Team of Champions, believes "a commitment to people development is what separates good leaders from great leaders" (6). A few authors who provide significant insight into the explanation of the effectiveness of servant leadership are Warren Bennis, Peter Block, Stephen Covey, Max DePree, James Kouzes, and Peter Senge, to name a few. These authors provide suggested approaches that are unique and applicable for organizations, whether religious or secular. Servant leadership aligns with character because both are who you are as a leader. Now the question that comes to mind is whether you can become a servant leader if you do not believe this is your particular leadership style. The answer is not easy because it calls for an examination of your character and your willingness to serve others first. The late renowned civil rights leader Mahatma Gandhi believed the best way for you to find yourself is to lose yourself through serving others. The first time I read this quote, I was also serving as a leader in a military organization as the logistics officer; the commander did the very thing Gandhi stated, he gave each of us undivided attention because he believed in our potential and wanted each of us to excel. The leader of the organization desired for each of us to get promoted to the next military rank and to be recognized for our efforts to help others as well.

I firmly believe, when serving others, your focus is no longer on self but on what is needed to assist another to reach his or her intended goal or achieve an accomplishment. Serving others is humbling and allows you to see a different perspective in another's thoughts, actions, behaviors, and values. Serving others can be instrumental in discovering truths about yourself, realizing how well off you are and what you have to offer others.

James Kouzes and Barry Posner (2012), authors of *The Leadership Challenge: How to Make Extraordinary Things Happen in Organizations*, conducted a survey from 1987 to 2012 and developed a list of what others believe are the admired and expected personal traits, characteristics, and attributes of leaders. The list was narrowed down to twenty characteristics of admired leaders, with the top characteristics being honesty, forward-looking, competency, and inspiring. Competency is the one characteristic most look for in leaders because it speaks to a follower's desire to follow. Kouzes and Posner's (2012) "Five Practices of Exemplary Leadership" is an example of how leaders who serve others empower and are considered to be those who desire the best for others.

The character of a servant leader begins with the leader and how he/she conducts himself/herself consistently without fanfare. Some servant leaders have the propensity to revolve from where they used to reside, in regard to behaviors and actions, through a mind-set change or, as many prefer, a paradigm shift. When you meditate on the characteristics of a servant leader, picture them like pearls. A pearl symbolizes wisdom acquired through experience. Peter Northouse's (2013) book *Leadership: Theory and Practice* supports and agrees with Larry Spear's (2010), CEO of the Greenleaf Center for Servant Leadership, summation of the ten strands or characteristics of a servant leader. The list that is mentioned by Northouse and Spear is not exhaustive; the additional traits are listening, empathy, healing, awareness, persuasion, conceptualization, foresight, stewardship, growth, and building community. Listening to servant leaders is hearing the needs of the group or person. Listening helps in understanding the viewpoint of another. The servant leader in a Christian-based setting listens for direction from the Holy Spirit (inner voice of reasoning and prompting) when asking questions, which is instrumental when reflections occur for the sake of growth within the leader. Empathy is a vital characteristic because it can accept and recognize the uniqueness of spirit in others and not allow an adverse action to judge or to group everyone as the same. Empathy comes from a place of understanding or, as Peter Northouse (2013) suggests, is basically "standing in the shoes" (221) and demonstrating a genuine sense of knowing what a person is experiencing. Healing is making things whole but being supportive while considering the past, reviewing introspectively regarding the present, and assisting in considering new behaviors for the future. Healing is a healthy process for both the leader and follower.

Awareness, as well as self-awareness, is critical in attuning the servant leaders to the environment in which they are operating and assists in understanding self and how it affects others' ethics, values, and power. Awareness in servant leaders causes them to look at their blind spots to prevent unethical decisions. Servant leaders also understand how persuasion through clear communication that is intended on building a consensus is paramount. Conceptualization is merely the ability to be a visionary; this is primarily seeing the big picture, which is instrumental in instilling possibilities for what is ahead and in developing plans. Servant leaders understand and recognize how foresight and conceptualization are similar. However, foresight looks at and understand lessons from the past, while observing and taking current situations into consideration, all while developing or predicting future occurrences derived from collected and/or observed data. Servant leaders view and uphold stewardship as a trust in the position they hold as leaders to do the right thing.

Stewardship is managing others and resources while remaining focused on service to others first. Servant leaders committed to the growth of people take into consideration the intrinsic values of others that overshadow substantial contributions in or for an organization. Servant leaders view building community through collective collaboration of personnel who have shared interests for the sake of unity, which is higher than individual interests. Servant leaders see building community as a means of bringing together like interests for a higher outcome.

COMPETENCIES OF A COACH

Coaching competencies are critical and essential to the success of both the coach and coachee. Coaching competencies, like character, are essential, and without them, harm or lack of growth in reaching an individual's maximum potential is at risk. Coaching requires a range of skills as well as knowledge. It is essential for coaches to be competent in working with coachees who may have a different background than their own. This requires the coach to possess both emotional and social intelligence, according to the authors of

Handbook of Coaching Psychology: A Guide for Practitioners, Stephen Palmer and Alison Whybrow (2011). The International Coach Federation believes there are eleven competencies in coaching. The eleven core coaching competencies are grouped into four clusters. The competencies are not weighted or prioritized, and all provide a greater understanding about various skills and approaches used within today's coaching profession. Defined by the International Coach Federation (ICF) these competencies are as follows: First, *setting the foundation*, which includes (1) meeting ethical guidelines and professional standards by understanding established coaching ethics and standards and applying them to coaching situations; and (2) establishing the coaching agreement—this occurs by creating an understanding of what is required during coaching engagements and having a set agreement with the coachee. Second, *co-creating the relationship* by (3) establishing trust and intimacy with the client through a safe and conducive environment, fostering a mutual level of trust and respect from the coachee; and (4) having a coaching presence that is attentive, spontaneous, and provides the coachee with your physical and mental awareness. Third, *communicate effectively* by (5) active listening, by being wholly focused on the coachee's verbal and nonverbal cues (for what is not being said); (6) asking powerful questions that require explanations and assist in maximizing coaching efforts; and (7) having direct communication, which occurs when there is a compelling dialogue during engagements, leading to impact and clarity. Finally, *facilitate learning and results* through (8) creating awareness by integrating information to assist the coachee in obtaining or gaining awareness toward actions or behaviors and developing alternative methods to counter previous reactions; (9) designing actions in introducing or creating opportunities, which lead to other possibilities for work and life; (10) planning and goal setting, which occur through the coachee's actions, to create a realistic plan of action to reach goals; and (11) managing progress and accountability by recognizing what is essential to the coachee and holding him or her responsible for the actions.

GODLY CHARACTER

What is a godly character, and does it matter if you have one? Serving in a position of authority in a Christian organization calls for an individual's character to resemble one who is approachable, knowledgeable, humble, empathetic, and, above all, trusting and honest. The Bible is full of lessons and stories about leadership and character. Nehemiah is one of the Old Testament historical books that provides instructions for leaders. Let's recall a few things regarding Nehemiah. He was cupbearer for King Artaxerxes of Persia, and through prayer, petition, and favor, he was released to rebuild a wall in Jerusalem, which had been destroyed over 140 years earlier, but he also restored faith in exiled Israel, which was over eight hundred miles away. Why am I restating the story from the Bible? Sometimes we need to recall occurrences to understand the cause of something and to establish a new approach in maximizing the potential of and in individuals who are willing and able to change past behaviors or actions.

Nehemiah teaches character in godly leadership as well as the capacity to approach God-sized quandaries and provide possibilities for what seems impractical, regarding situations to the nonbelieving leader. Godly leaders are often men and women who have changed due to encounters, maturity, or a significant emotional event (SEE) and are now encouraging, transforming, transparent agents of change. Remember Nehemiah was not in the same location of the situation (the wall in Jerusalem), but because of need, desire, and his servant heart, he decided to do what was in him: serve for the greater good of others. Nehemiah did not have to give up the comforts of being the king's cupbearer, a position that afforded him with the best of everything, but he could not simply sit by and allow the people to suffer at the hands of their enemy.

Spiritual leaders, especially Christians, understand God's desire is to develop leaders after His heart for the sake of rebuilding and renewing faith in nations, churches, families, and individuals who are removed from Him because of circumstances or to bring new converts to know Him. Godly leaders carry a message of hope and encouragement and usually walk in love. Spiritual leaders under whom I have sat have explained that the reason they are where they are is due to being broken. Being broken from the past changed their characters, and in return, they are better leaders who understand the need to serve and to leave past disappointments, deceptions, and betrayals behind and to become the men or women God called them to be by serving without looking for a return. The character of Jesus quickens and causes a shift, which provides clarity and walks not in clouded judgment. Galatians 6:1 reminds believers, "Brethren, even if a man be overtaken in any trespass, ye which is spiritual, restore such a one in a spirit of meekness; looking to thyself, lest you too be tempted" (ESV). This just means no one is independent, and as a leader, it is important to remember it is his or her responsibility to assist in serving others.

Godly character rebuilds, renews, and encourages. Leaders show concern and respond to situations based on factual information. The leader then becomes either empathetic or sympathetic; this is modern-day social and emotional intelligence, which assists in understanding culture. Nehemiah is an example of a leader with godly character. He answered the call to help in correcting a problem that had existed for well over 140 years. His desire to serve was for the greater good of others. He asked direct questions for the sake of clarity and to ensure others around him had an understanding of the task in building the wall. Nehemiah facilitated learning and results through awareness, worked to incite the need for action toward results, and saw the need for realistic, attainable, and managed progress.

▎TAKEAWAYS

The character of a leader also aligns with the core competencies of a coach suggested by ICF. Your character is who you are; your competencies are learned and acquired formally and informally. The Bible is full of lessons and stories about leadership and character. It is important to remember that as a leader, others have a higher expectation of your character and competencies. Influence is the core reason character and competency are essential in leadership. A coaching relationship will not occur if a coachee does not feel safe or if there is a lack of trust. Your character is who you are, and your abilities provide the coachee with confidence as he or she looks to you to provide influence through guidance and partnership.

CHAPTER 7
Coaching Is Servant Leadership

Do nothing from selfish ambition or conceit, but, in
humility count others more significant than ourselves.
—Philippians 2:3 (ESV)

A leader takes people where they want to go. A great leader
takes people where they don't want to go, but ought to be.
—Rosalynn Carter

Former First Lady Rosalynn Carter, an advocate of empowering others, believed a great leader assists other in reaching great potential by supporting them in seeing both the possibilities and plausibility in their situations. Her influence and perspective reminded me of a method of helping to take others to the next level, developed by John Whitmore (2009), named the GROW sequence, which includes **G**oal **R**eality **O**ptions **W**hat, when, whom, will principle. This principle allows an individual to realistically look at a goal and develop strategies to achieve them.

This final chapter will summarize and connect previous chapters. I will address what coaching is and why it is crucial, the importance of the coaching relationship, the importance of assessments, the differences in coaching and teaching, and how leadership theories and styles are affected by coaching. I will describe the characteristics and competencies of a leader and coach, what is servant leadership, and, finally, how coaching is servant leadership. Throughout these discussions, the lighthouse that I will be guiding toward leads back to serving, empowering, encouraging, motivating, listening, asking the powerful questions, direct communication, and accountability. You will discover that everything previously discussed is centered on servant leadership and coaching.

When you are the appointed leader or are thrust into a leadership position, does the following question ever cross your mind (faith-based or non–faith-based): What does God (or perhaps the organization) have in store for me? When I was seeking inspiration from the types of leaders who had a desire to assist and change the outcome of many, research led me to the Bible. Biblical servant leaders worth noting include Abraham, Joseph, Moses, Joshua, Nehemiah, David, Daniel, Esther, Christ, Paul, Peter, and even a mere shepherd (this is not an exhaustive list). These servant leaders displayed the characteristics described by Robert Greenleaf (2002), the pioneer of servant leadership. Inspired by Peter Northouse (2013), these elements of a servant leader include listening, demonstrating empathy, understanding that healing is essential to the wholeness of the individual, possessing self-awareness, possessing persuasion, conceptualizing the big picture, possessing foresight, understanding stewardship, empowering others to be accountable for their actions, and commitment to developing others and building communities.

Servant leaders are those who desire and understand it is their task to assist others and allow them to decide how they plan to achieve their goals. After all, each person has individual desires or goals, and many understand it will require work to achieve them. Every one of the previously mentioned characteristics of leaders starts with a desire to assist, paired with action for others and less for self. A leader is one who influences others, rather than merely seeking out followers.

Developing others begins with an individual's desire to change, and you, as a leader, then partner with that individual for the purpose of change. Coaching is more than providing a service to others; coaching is servant leadership! Some believe coaching is merely for executives in places of significant influence, but coaching is for everyone. When referring to coaching, it is important to note athletic coaching is different from personal coaching, which involves life, career, performance, and behavior. I mention athletic coaching because, too often, this technique or style comes to mind when someone says he or she has a coach. Their coach is there to assist them in moving from where they are to where they desire to be. A personal coach is not in the business of telling an individual or team what they need to do. Some athletic coaches walk in a broader sense of the role of coach, allowing the players to make moves, then asking questions before correcting the players on what they should do. This is when the coach becomes a teacher or mentor. Coaching is recognizing an opening for another to be creative and innovative and then encouraging the coachee to have faith and believe in what he or she is called to do.

I question the individuals who firmly believe coaching does not belong in the church; it leaves me to think we are not growing leaders in faith-based organizations the way leaders are grown in secular organizations. When there is no growth among leaders in religious organizations, leaders typically operate in the status quo or traditions of what has occurred for years. Observation and experience have afforded me the opportunity to witness disgruntled leaders in the church, and it leads to a questioning of their purpose within the congregation or to second-guess their calling based on what is not occurring in regard to spiritual growth. When there is growth in non–faith-based organizations, individuals usually are developed for positions of greater responsibility or to increase and strengthen performance, which leads to improving behavior.

Throughout this work, I was compelled to share my experiences and observations, not from the standpoint of sounding as if I have done it all but that I have been a constant learner all of my life. When I was young, a high school counselor ill advised me (in my opinion) to go to vocational school. (There is nothing wrong with vocational education, but it was not the best route for me.) I thought the counselor believed vocational training was my best route after taking my circumstances into consideration, but she did not see the potential within me. When I look back at this advice, I think she may have believed it was mentoring. My belief in my potential to serve others, however, outweighed her perceived sound judgment. What is in an individual is usually because of environmental influences or culture, and we as servant leaders have the potential to assist others in reshaping their lives and to help them reach their potential.

An individual's culture often influences decisions. I have learned from studying the works of Edgar H. Schein, PhD (2010), author of *Organizational Culture and Leadership*, who believes organizational culture is continuously recreated and lived by interactions with others and is shaped by our behaviors. Schein's research findings and suggestions explain why some faith-based organizations do not desire to introduce coaching: The mind-set of the culture can heavily influence decision making and behaviors. Shein's statement regarding culture can sometimes drive the order and support by the actions of individual toward specific organizational processes, procedures, practices, and values. At the risk of sounding forward, coaching is not a new practice; it has been around (as was mentioned in chapter 1) since the beginning of time. At its inception, it was not labeled as coaching. Kim Cameron and Robert Quinn (2011), authors of *Diagnosing and Changing Organizational Culture*, believe there is a dire need to manage organizational culture, as change is pervasive and no successful organization remains the same and continues to grow. In other words, Cameron and Quinn believe that in the midst of organizational challenges, it is not a question of *if* they will change but *when*, for the sake of being relevant.

Furthermore, coaches do not need to possess all the skills of a coachee to be effective. To drive my point, Andy Stanley, author of *Next Generation Leader,* reminds his readers of two vital points from an experience: (1) you can go further and faster with a coach than you can on your own, and (2) a competent coach does not have to possess more skills than the coachee. A professional coach is a significant investment, and it is not about the capabilities of the coach but instead his or her desire to serve others. Leadership is packed with pressure, and it calls for leaders to think fast on their feet.

One of the challenges leaders face is developing and growing leaders in faith-based and non–faith-based organizations alike.

Philippians 2:3–5 states, "Do nothing from rivalry or conceit, but in humility count others more significant than yourselves. Let each of you look not only to his own interests but also to the interests of others" (ESV). Paul's example of Christ's humility was a message to the Philippians and a reminder to believers today, especially those in leadership, to love one another and work together, demonstrating the importance of putting others first. Philippians 2:3–5 is an example of the qualities of a servant and an exemplary leader. The authors of *The Leadership Challenge,* James Kouzes and Barry Posner (2012), focus attention on what they have coined as five practices of exemplary leadership, which include (1) model the way, (2) inspire a shared vision, (3) challenge the process, (4) enable others to act, and (5) encourage the heart. These five practices are what servant leadership and coaching is all about. First, modeling the way includes remembering that a title is not what makes you a leader; rather, it's taking the initiative to make things happen. The effective leader models the ability to work toward a goal, to articulate values and principles to govern one's actions, and to communicate what you expect of others. Second, inspiring a shared vision informs others of aspirations, which allows others to develop their own in alignment and strategic fit with the collective purpose. When leaders inspire a shared vision, they facilitate change, and this encourages creativity, innovation, and flexibility. Third, when leaders challenge processes, they demonstrate that status quo is not the standard, and the challenge is not to question your skills, knowledge, experience, or behaviors but to get to the root of the reasoning of logic. Fourth, when leaders enable others to act, there is a collaborative atmosphere. When a leader allows others to lead on his or her approved ideas, this empowers them. Enabling others fosters collaboration and also inspires cross-training, which strengthens confidence and competencies and increases self-determination. Finally, encouraging the heart occurs when others are recognized, cheered on, and rewarded for what they accomplish toward change because of the collective commitment to improve current situations. The five practices of exemplary leadership set aside self and focus on the good of others because of one's desire to serve.

▌SERVANT LEADER

In chapter 5, I briefly discussed several leadership styles to include servant leadership. Servant leadership should be an accepted leadership style in the body of believers, but we know this is not always the case. Skills, characteristics, traits, and competencies of servant leaders or servant leadership are parallel to coaching; the common denominator is the individual who is present and who assists others in reaching their goals, desires, or calling by asking thought-provoking questions. I use the term *calling* because members in faith-based organizations understand the call of their lives to serve but sometimes without asking for help first from the Holy Spirit. We are reminded of our need for kingdom guidance in Matthew 6:33. "But seek first the kingdom of God and His righteousness, and these things will be added to you" (ESV).

I stated earlier that I cannot recall how many times I have heard a faith-based leader, speaking from the pulpit or in a meeting, say words that sounds like a chorus, "I am a servant leader!" Servant leaders also take care of their leaders. Servant leaders understand the importance of asking questions for the sake of assisting another person with desires and wants. Servant leaders also understand individuals' needs come from God, according to Philippians 4:19. "And my God shall supply every need of yours according to his riches in glory in Christ Jesus" (ESV). Coaching leaders foster learning, development, and increased confidence in the individual's calling. Throughout this book, it has been my desire for faith-based leaders to understand and hear how serving forward is a form of connection between God, the coach, and the coachee. Coaching other leaders is the soil where the seed (individual), which God has placed in the faith-based leader's care to nurture, grows through questioning and provides them a place to talk aloud.

As a leader who has served and is currently serving in the church, it is hard to sit back and watch other lay leaders not reach their full potential or capacity in their different roles and responsibilities in the church, just because the faith-based leader does not understand the value or benefits of coaching. He or she may not believe coaching is necessary for the church, merely because it is not mentioned by name in the Bible. Coaching does not occur in some churches because the leader does not have the time or the skills to coach his or her lay leaders. As well, some faith-based leaders are skeptical when it comes to coaching; it appears to be a form of business. Some simply perceive coaching in the sense of sports, rather than leadership development, due to inaccurate understanding.

Jesus is considered as the most excellent servant leader ever, but not every faith-based leader or Christian demonstrates the behaviors of a servant leader. First Thessalonians 5:12–13 states, "We ask you, brothers, to respect those who labor among you and are over you and the Lord and admonish you, and to assisting them very highly in love because of their work. Be at peace among yourselves" (ESV). Servant leadership causes others to be happier and more productive.

ROBERT GREENLEAF

Leaders such as Larry C. Spears (2010), the president and CEO of Larry C. Spears Center for Servant Leadership, credits the 1970s introduction of servant leadership to Robert Greenleaf. Robert Greenleaf had a storied career in research, management, development, and education for thirty-eight years for Atlantic Telephone & Telegraph (AT&T) before retiring in 1964 and beginning his second and most rewarding career as a writer, consultant, and teacher. Greenleaf stood on the principle that the best leaders are servants first, and essential tools for a servant leader include active listening, persuasion of one's desires, access to intuition and foresight, use of clear language, and practical measurement of outcomes.

Greenleaf (2002) conceived servant leadership after reading Hermann Hesse's (1956) novel *The Journey to the East.* In the story, a group of men set off on a journey, all of whom have goals or reasons why the mission is essential to them. There is a servant with them named Leo; he performs necessary chores but has an impact on day-to-day functions. Leo is described as one with wisdom, great humor, full of songs, enthusiastic, and encouraging. Leo's presence is instrumental to the travelers, causing them to sojourn without issues, until one day when he disappears. Through their discovery of many things, they soon realize how much Leo did for them; without him, this task of traveling becomes arduous. After a while, they desert the journey. The men realize the servant was the real leader through his selflessness. Years later, one of the journeymen finds Leo and discovers he was indeed the group's leader in the league in which they were seeking membership.

Robert Greenleaf (2002) primarily points to a critical takeaway to Hermann Hesse's novel: Great leaders are first great servants who focus on the needs of others, and they are not always recognized as the servants for their work. Servant leaders do more than adhere to the requirements of others; they are forward thinkers with prophetic insights. Servant leaders understand the lack of others and are willing to assist them to achieve their desired goals by asking thought-provoking questions. Servant leaders are attentive to their followers, have empathy, and are natural nurturers.

Five modern-day servant leaders who recognized and led by placing the needs of others ahead of their own are Martin Luther King Jr., Nelson Mandela, Mahatma Gandhi, Mother Teresa, and Albert Schweitzer. These leaders saw a need, had faith, desired better for others, and did not seek personal gain. Service to others was what pleased them. The five leaders were faith-based and had faith in knowing that, yes, they were leaders, but also, they were better followers (servants) first. Dr. Albert Schweitzer reminds us, "I don't know what your destiny will be, but one thing I do know: the only ones among us who will be happy are those who have sought and found how to serve" (Roach 2014).

It is interesting that Jesus talked about being a servant to James and John, the sons of Zebedee. James and John did not understand what they were asking when they asked Jesus to grant them special positions of honor in His kingdom. Jesus questioned their motives in Mark 10:35–40 by telling them they did not know what they were asking. He then asked them if they could do what he did. Jesus reminded James and John that to be great, one must first serve, and He (Jesus) did not come for others to serve His needs but for Him to assist them in meeting their requirement. In Matthew 5, when Jesus gives the Sermon on the Mount, He reminds the people they are both salt and light. Jesus allows them to know their value is in affecting the world. On any given Sunday, Christians gather to worship; at that time, there is an enormous amount of salt and light. When individuals are outside of the church walls, the salt and light that resides in them should saturate the world.

LEADERSHIP DEFINED

The definition of leadership is centered on influence. Peter Northouse, PhD (2013), professor emeritus at Western Michigan University, consultant, and author of *Leadership: Theory and Practice*, summarizes an essential point regarding leadership: It is a highly valued phenomenon and is complicated in the way it influences people and affects outcomes. Northouse further believes leadership includes attention to shared goals, and leaders are morally responsible for knowing the needs and concerns of followers. Leadership is also a process, not a trait or character within a leader; instead, it is the result of a transactional event that occurs between the leader and follower.

What is leadership, and why does it vex consultants, organizational leaders, and lay people? Kevin Kruse (2015), a contributing author to *Forbes* magazine, defines and believes leadership is a process of social influence that maximizes the efforts of others toward the achievement of a goal. Let us begin with what leadership is not. Leadership has nothing to do with the senior person in charge of an organization. Leadership is not in a title or in personal attributes.

Leadership is defined in many ways, but most dictionaries and professionals narrow it down to maximizing influence. I can imagine what you are thinking: *I do not need another lesson on servant leadership. After all, this is what I am doing.* My question is, Are you a servant leader or another kind of leader? I have met some who believe they are transformational or charismatic leaders instead of servant leaders because of the lives they are changing. I offer this to think about: how important it is to empower and put the needs of others before you because it is in you.

‖SERVANT LEADER AND FOLLOWER

Peter Northouse (2013) suggests servant leadership appears paradoxical because it is an approach to leadership that runs counter to common sense. Why is the walk of servant leader still not fully understood in many organizations? It is essential to clear up the misconception of servant leaders and servant leadership. I can recall hearing one faith-based leader repeatedly say, "We are a servant church, and I am a servant leader!" When I hear this, I remember the pioneer of servant leadership, Robert Greenleaf (2002), repeating the words of Jesus the Christ—that a good leader must first be a good servant.

It is important to have a clear understanding of what a servant does and who a servant is. In my experience with church, a leader who says, "I am a servant leader," often is repeating prior demonstrations and following tradition or cultural understanding, all which leads to operating within limitations. I was a member of a large church that frequently reminded us that Pastor was a servant leader. All I ever witnessed in that church was the leader surrounded by those whom I referred to as "pectoral guards"; he left soon after quickly greeting new members or visitors, off to prepare for the next service. I never witnessed him or his wife interacting with any of the people past the designated leaders' row. The leaders in the first two rows were a copy of his leadership style; seldom did they interact with congregants. My observations led me to believe many leaders have the wrong definition of servant leaders or servant leadership. Many of the leaders followed the thought of taking care of the widows, elders, and those in need mentally, physically, and financially. Many operated under the auspices of Jesus the Christ as the ultimate servant leader, and He is, but many still do not understand Jesus's demonstrations of being a servant. Being a servant leader, however, is not just doing for others. Servant leaders serve because of their desire. A servant leader as a coach is one who spends time understanding the needs of other leaders who serve in the organization and who brings the best out of them, resulting in their wanting to be that type of leader as well.

Let us look at Robert Greenleaf's (2002) example of a servant leader before going back to review an actual and ultimate servant leader, Jesus. Leaders know how to influence, and servants know how to follow! In the book of Mark, Jesus's preparation of the disciples is the most excellent example of a servant leader. Many will agree when Jesus healed the sick and infirm, raised the dead, transformed lives, and brought what we consider today as social consciousness through teaching against the exclusion of others (he placed the needs of others first), this made Him a servant leader. Yes, everything previously mentioned is what a servant leader does, and Jesus's legacy remained with the disciples, who marveled at the miraculous teaching and works of Christ while He walked with them and after His departure. The disciples desired to serve as Jesus did. The disciples marveled and asked questions when they were alone with Jesus because they did not fully understand. Jesus served them by explaining and continuing to allow them to see what He meant by serving others.

When reviewing the book of Mark, we are reminded of the discussion the disciples had while traveling through Galilee. When they reached Capernaum, Jesus asked them, "What were you arguing about on the road?" (Mark 9:33). When the disciples gave up everything and began to follow Jesus, their human side and Jewish lineage caused them to discuss rank and order. John Walvoord and Roy Zuck (2004), authors of The Bible Knowledge Commentary, believe during their argument, the human side (Jews) argued about who had the most significant position in the messianic kingdom. Their misguided understanding of what each one was called to do allowed Jesus to know the disciples still did not know His passion. In Mark 9:34–35, we read,

> But they kept silent, for on the way they had argued with one another about who was the greatest. And he sat down and called the twelve. And he said to them, "If anyone would be first, he must be last of all and servant of all." (ESV)

Jesus sat down with the disciples and taught them the importance of sitting in the highest position. He had to deliberately take the lowest place and take care of the needs of others by being a servant. It is not ironic, nor is it written that their seeking an improved position offended Jesus. He was a coach, mentor, and teacher. Jesus encouraged the disciples to ask questions, just as He asked them thought-provoking questions that caused them to think about what they currently knew and to begin to think of what was possible. Jesus further explained He did not determine their place of honor. Greatness in His kingdom is defined by service, not status. When we consider the importance of a servant leader, it bears repeating the name and reading the research of Robert Greenleaf, the pioneer behind the revolutionary coined phrase servant-leader or servant leader.

Leading as a servant leader in the church empowers members, as well those serving in leadership positions, to be salt and light in the church as well as outside the church. How is it possible? Imagine you are coaching, or perhaps an external professional coach is coaching your appointed leaders. What he or she is learning to do in the decision-making process causes a mind-set shift spiritually, personally, and professionally. The noticeable change has the proclivity to cause others to change how they are thinking, which creates a mind-set shift. As a servant leader, your attitude can cause those around you to want to lead like you because they know goals, questions, and actions produce changes that alter the atmosphere; this is how salt and light spill into the workplace and the world.

Servant leadership challenges traditional understanding regarding leadership; its approach is both unique and rewarding. I am interjecting the thought of followership as part of servant leadership. Followership is congruent to servant leadership by supporting the desires of others as subordinates. Contributing *Harvard Business Review* author Robert Kelly (1998) of "In Praise of Followers," illuminates an overlooked occurrence in leadership: followers. The concept of a follower is often overlooked because the greater emphasis is in the study of leaders or leadership, with little to no consideration focused on those who ensure the mission, task, or idea materializes into existence. Kelly illuminated the point that an organization is either successful or fails, based on two factors: leaders and followers. The individual in an organization who takes pleasure in mission accomplishment is a follower who operates with different motivations that lead to success for the greater good. Effective followers are innovative and creative in finding ways to assist the leader to achieve. Think about this notion: Most of us are natural followers because all of us answer to someone. Being a follower is a dominant part of life. However, there is more significant attention and emphasis on leadership. When you take a step back and look at what we are doing on a day-to-day basis, it's often not the aspects of leadership but the actions of a follower. Efficient followers are individuals who can manage themselves well, are committed to an organization, build competencies, and focus on maximum output. Such persons are also credible, courageous, and honest.

The other distinguishing qualities of an active follower are self-reliant participation, enthusiasm, and intelligence. They are also aware of how others follow, which motivates them to support those who are submissive and supportive of senior leadership. The three previously mentioned qualities are based on the follower's motivation and the context of what he or she desires. In other words, followers view what they are doing in various ways, such as being a team player and supporting a cause, product, project, or service. Robert Kelly further highlights the characteristics of a follower with wrong motives, one who does not view followership as alluring but establishes his or her stance for the sake of being noticed. The follower in this vein desires to win the confidence of supervisors and peers, which possibly leads to moving up the corporate ladder. Critical factors to assess in followers are their motivations, perceptions, and desired gain.

▌SERVANT LEADERSHIP AND COACHING

Do nothing from selfish ambition or conceit, but in
humility count others more significant than ourselves.
—Philippians 2:3 (ESV)

In order to understand how servant leadership is coaching (or vice versa) and how there are similarities, it is crucial to re-associate oneself with the definition of leadership and review servant leadership from a theoretical approach. There is academic nullification regarding the effectiveness of servant leadership, mainly because of skepticism and lack of understanding of the variables, such as service, trust, humility, and influence. Such traits carry the burden of motivating others to do more, based on their values and beliefs. The values of a servant leader are often different than the values of a non-servant leader because of the leader's focus on service to others instead of the organization. When we review the focus of a servant leader and those of a coach, there are more significant similar variables than with any other leadership theory. Servant leadership is often taken from the context of the leadership of Jesus. The servant leadership of Jesus is accessible and makes a difference in the world through caring and loving your neighbor as yourself. Coaching is servant leadership because it exhibits a willingness to serve and focus on the desires of others. Various research findings are supportive of Dr. Kathleen Patterson (2003), author and professor, whose theories regarding servant leadership provide a greater understanding and focus on the faith-based aspects of servant leadership in its characteristics and constructs. In Dr. Patterson's article "Servant Leadership: A Theoretical Model," she describes the construct of service of a servant leader: (1) agapao love, (2) humility, (3) altruism, (4) vision, (5) trust, (6) empowerment, and (7) service.

A brief explanation of the previously mentioned constructs will provide clarity to how effective each is in servant leadership. Agapao love is the type of love Robert Greenleaf (2002) describes in *Servant Leadership: A Journey into the Nature of Legitimate Power & Greatness* as an indefinable term, in that it has infinite manifestations. *Agapao love* is a moral love (encouraging goodness and decency). Agapao love is a driver within servant leaders because the focus is on the whole person. The Christian Bible Reference website describes *humility* as being respectful of others; in Patterson's findings, she illuminates humility as a virtue that rejects self or own merits. Humility causes one to listen to others, which leads to ways to better serve others, rather than promoting one's own agenda. Jim Collins (2001), author of *Good to Great*, believes humility in leaders is often underestimated because of one's desire to assist others to succeed instead of self. *Altruism* is based on good motives and behavior for the sake of helping others. *Vision* in servant leadership focuses on the future of others within the organization. Servant leadership looks at where individual desires ought to be, which leads to development and thought-provoking questions regarding the follower's plan of action. *Trust* occurs when there is integrity and demonstrates an authentic concern for others. Trust is what Peter Northouse (2013) describes as being predictable in situations that are unpredictable, and Patterson finds trust a building block for servant leaders. Trust is servant leadership—doing what you say you are going to do, which builds empowered followers. *Empowerment* occurs when servant leaders listen, and others feel significant because of value placed on what is communicated. Empowerment is assisting followers in finding their paths toward growth and allowing them to steer the course while balancing development. *Service* to others is what servant leaders do when they authentically give.

Dr. Patterson highlights service through compassion, time, care, energy, and sometimes belonging, if it assists in propelling a follower to a better place. These mentioned constructs provide a perspective

DR. ANITA S. GREENLEE

of the innate behaviors and attitudes consistent with the focus of followers (or when you consider coaching, the coachee) pervading a service to others. When reviewing the core competencies of coaching and the constructs of servant leadership, they are virtually the same. Dr. Patterson (2003) advocates that servant leadership's seven virtuous constructs work in a processional pattern (beginning with agapao love and ending with service). When operating within the core competencies of coaching, a processional order may appear disruptive to the coachee's agenda, but the coach may find it instrumental once the foundation is established, and there is a relationship that aids efficient communication and facilitates learning and results.

Research findings of Gregory Stone, Robert Russell, and Kathleen Patterson (2004), in *The Leadership & Organizational Development Journal in Transformational Versus Servant Leadership: A Difference in Leader Focus*, provide similarities as well as differences of transformational leadership and servant leadership, with foci on what one does and how the other affects people. To ensure clarity and to rest the theory that they are essentially the same, transformational leadership focus is organizational, and the higher good and servant leadership focus is on people/followers. Repeats of credit belong to Robert Greenleaf (2002), the initiator of servant leadership, whose beliefs rest in the notion that leadership meets the needs of others, not self. Stone, et.al., illuminate Greenleaf's premise that servant leaders develop individuals who flourish, provide vision, gain credibility and trust, and influence others. There are many similarities in the attributes of servant leaders and the characteristics of coaching.

Servant leaders and coaches display the same focus to empower others. Coaches and servant leaders focus on service to others. Stone, Russell, and Patterson further illuminate the resonating importance of servant leaders and coaches and believe relationship and empowerment take precedence over one's desires. It is also important to remember the agenda belongs to the follower or coachee.

COACHING FITS YOUR LEADERSHIP DEVELOPMENT PLAN

What does your organizational or individual leadership development plan look like? Is the plan labeled as coaching but is saturated with mentoring? Mentoring is not coaching! As a coach, I understand the difference between the two and also the distinct discrepancies that lie within what both do regarding serving others. I am not dismissing that one does not embody servant leadership, but there are differences that should be considered in regard to what is needed in the organization.

I remember conducting a seminar and asking the question, "What do you and your organization need? Do you need a mentor, teacher, or coach?" The intent of these questions was to cause the business owners to assess what was needed and why. The developmental plan you choose for you or your organization makes a difference. There is a need for both coaching and mentoring in different environments, but when you look at the bottom line up front (BLUF), coaching is the discovery and awakening to an individual's personality, communication skills, strengths, and leadership style, and it assists in understanding one's governing theories and decision-making processes.

A mentor, on the other hand, conveys and presents options as well as sharing his or her experiences for growth. Psalms 34:7 reminds us, "Delight yourself in the Lord, and He will give you the desires of your heart" (ESV). Some leaders in faith-based organizations understand that to delight in someone or something, a connection must occur, which often leads to a relationship. Trusting in God includes a trust in the plans He foreknew before the foundations of the earth. Jeremiah 29:11 also reminds us of this truth: "For I know the plans I have for you, declares the Lord, plans for welfare and not for evil, to give you a future and a hope" (ESV). The scripture strengthens a believer's faith that if God has a plan, then there is a possibility that I, as a leader, can help encourage this plan in the lives of others. Leaders who encourage others to move forward in their goals and plans do so by supporting and providing them with the resources within their scope. Such leaders understand what it means to serve.

Coaching must find its place within your organizational development plan and your leadership. Leaders and emerging leaders do not realize the scrutiny with which others continuously assess their behavior, performance, skills, and knowledge from the first day they show up in their roles. The responsibility of a leader can be arduous and at the same time humbling because a leader is called to serve. The role of a leader in developing others begins with confidence and security in his or her skills, competencies, and experiences. From there, one must possess a desire to grow and develop others.

Leadership-development plans involve assessing and ascertaining the right fit and what is beneficial for either a person or an organization. Leadership is influence; this influence occurs in an environment in which there is awareness of who are the personnel and leaders and what skills among them are abundant or lacking. Once there is clarity of these elements, feedback can be offered regarding why the organization is operating in the capacity that it is and what you can do to serve them. One way to serve others is to introduce leadership-development programs, such as coaching. I caution leaders who desire to present coaching to the organization to first assess the organization's readiness for coaching. Coaching is no longer an executive-only tool for developing; it can and should be a tool that improves, changes, and reshapes organizational and individual processes, performances, behaviors, and decision making. An organizational coaching assessment (OCA) assists leaders or decision-makers when considering whether the organization is prepared to introduce coaching initiatives. James Hunt and Joseph Weintraub (2007), authors of *The Coaching Organization*, suggest the organization's cultural context (what employees believe and value and what their assumptions are) is what drives an organization's success.

It is also important to remember coaching is a form of leadership development, and when leaders invest the time and resources necessary in their leadership pool, there will be noticeable intangible and tangible results. Coaching is a learning process that encourages the coachee to perceive what a potential outcome is, instead of referring to previous occurrences. Coaching can occur internally, but it is vital for the designated internal coach to have an understanding of the suggested core competencies and not turn coaching engagements into counseling sessions. Leadership-development plans are great tools to actively involve the individual who seeks to improve his or her performances, decision making, and behaviors. Ellen Van Velsor, Cynthia McCauley, and Marian Ruderman (2010), authors at the Center for Creative Leadership, believe leader development enlarges individuals' abilities to be effective in leadership, and the best development experiences are derived from assessment data.

COACHING AS A SERVANT LEADER IS RELATIONAL, NOT CONTROLLING

The best leader is the one who has sense enough to pick good
men to do what he wants to be done, and the self-restraint
to keep from meddling with them while they do it.
—Theodore Roosevelt

The coaching relationship is a dynamic partnership with a primary purpose that centers on trust, honesty, respect, and forward movement from the created awareness, leading to results. Former President Theodore Roosevelt recognized that the best leaders know themselves and are not intimidated by another talent that serves with them; they have the self-control not to interfere with the plans of the chosen individual. As a leader and coach, there is a constant reminder that coaching is present, which means actively listening and watching while remembering there is no magic formula for anything. In coaching, faith is the key, while deliberate forward actions cause changes to occur. The individual who has the desire to shift expends the effort, which leads to awareness and alterations. Kimsey-House, Kimsey-House, Sandahl, and Whitworth (2011), authors of *Co-Active*

Coaching, encourage leaders and coaches to remember that as a coach, you are engaging a person, not a problem that needs to be solved. The person has a situation to change or resolve or a task to accomplish, and as a coach or leader, you are partnering with him or her toward transformation. Within the coaching context, this is what is considered as focusing on the person, and it is a process that does not happen overnight. Relationships are enhanced as you coach and as you, as a leader, develop a greater understanding of the individual. This leads to trust and disclosure of intimate details from the coachee of his or her desires and plans. Gary Collins (2002) resounds the sentiments of Ken Blanchard, Bill Hybels, and Phil Hodges (2001) that the act of coaching is perhaps the most significant servant-leadership element in assisting others to accomplish their goals. Coaches seek to understand and value the importance of the persons they are serving through asking powerful questions and attentive listening. Such interaction provides reasoning to help design actions for the coachees. Coaching relationships are strengthened over time. During the relationship-building process, the coach demonstrates other servant-leadership behaviors, such as empowering the coachee and offering full autonomy in his or her decision-making process, which builds his or her confidence. The coaching relationship also requires a genuine coaching presence during engagements that are authentic and guided toward managing the progress of the coachee.

COACHING AND SERVANT LEADERS GROW AND REWRITE THE STORY

How many leadership development programs are you implementing with the same ineffective results because something is missing, or perhaps there are too many formalities, and the story remains the same? Coaching is not fun when there are too many formalities of process. Think about how we use creativity and develop appealing innovative strategies to motivate another person to learn and grow. The same is true when you are engaging and facilitating learning with a coachee. John Whitmore (2009), author of *Coaching for Performance*, suggests a model called GROW, which is useful when exploring new issues because it inspires the coachee to set a goal without considering the reality. While the process appears to put the cart before the horse, it encourages the coachee to establish both short- and long-term *goals*. The coachee then explores the *reality* of his or her current situation and develops solutions for the present while simultaneously exploring likely courses of action and strategies based on viable *options*, which is instrumental is answering *what* is required, *when* it is required, by *whom* it is required, and then stimulating free *will* to accomplish the goal. Coaches guide coachees through the process of looking at what is possible when they think past current and past performances and focus instead on an outcome and how it can be achieved. Servant leaders and leadership roles are about more than merely taking care of others outside of your organization in regard to survival needs. Servant leaders and leadership roles nurture organizational leaders who support the goals, mission, and vision of the organization. According to Peter Northouse (2013), author of *Leadership: Theory and Practice*, one of the characteristics of a servant leader is a commitment to the growth of others. James M. Burns (1978), author of *Leadership*, describes a leader who looks for potential in others as a transforming leader. Both types of leaders assist an individual in rewriting his or her story. The rewrite begins after engaging a solid assessment of the leader in focus. Such assessments are often a result of the organization or a multisource document that focuses on the strengths of the assessed.

Kenneth Jennings and John Stahl-Wert (2003), authors of *The Serving Leader*, remind readers that improvement occurs when they focus on strengths rather than weaknesses. In this environment, individuals assert and build on the advantages of the organization or individual, rather than the challenges. The message of Jennings and Stahl-Wert resounded the importance of ensuring the needs of others are attended to and that they are given solid consideration; this is what servant leaders do to empower others.

How does coaching rewrite the story? Coaching rewrites the story by shifting the assessment of where you currently are to where you desire to go, according to your realistic plan. Gary Collins (2002), author of *Christian Coaching*, reminds us that coaching assists in rewriting our stories through experience and practice. The story is rewritten because there are various discoveries and methods through the learning process that lead to different results than before. Stories are rewritten with the design of new actions, new plans, and establishing new goals. These actions and behaviors result in development of core competencies, skillfully facilitated by the coach in the life of the coachee.

REFLECTION: LOOKING IN THE MIRROR AND SEEING DIFFERENTLY

When I looked back at the past four years of being a student, it dawned on me how many of the professors were servants, mentors, and coaches. All of the professors were encouraging, were present in the moment, developed a rapport with each of us, actively listened, asked thought-provoking questions to get us to think past what we knew and to explore another view, and encouraged us to ask compelling questions of one another. Two professors consistently asked me what would happen to my discussions if I narrowed the scope and went deep. Although I did not realize it at the time, they were coaching me. Because of these conversations, I decided to take action that led to improvement in my communication with others. I firmly believe coaching is servant leadership, due to the nature of these leaders— their desire to serve, their presence, and their availability to others.

Robert Greenleaf's (2002) explanations led to a greater understanding that servant leaders are not looking for a reward for self but that the prize is watching and facilitating the growth, performance improvement, decision making, and behavior change in others' lives as they inspire new ways to accomplish a goal, plan, or task. I realized my shift into this model of servant leadership became evident during the third year of my doctoral program; this shift occurred after observing the need to ask the why and what of others for the sake of getting them to open themselves to possibilities.

I also realized another shift occurred while observing others as they reached their goals; we established a relationship, and I was their thinking partner.

I reflect back to my time in the military as a leader. It was an eye-opener and taught me a great deal of what a leader does and how imitation, or fake characteristics, are short-lived. It is essential to be authentic. As a cadet, I was instructed and mentored by wise leaders who understood that leadership is not about followers and ego; leadership is about influence and growing others. The military was also where I first cut my teeth on planning and ensuring what I desired was realistic. I remember hearing so many say that hope is not an option and planning is faith in what can happen. I mention this because coaching is teaching others to have faith in what they believe. The relationships I built with my soldiers have been long-lasting; some of them contact me still. No matter where they are in the world, their first question is whether I remember them. The call is usually to thank me for pushing them past where they were and to inform me that taking the time to listen and ask them questions made them explore possibilities, which made them a better leader. These individuals, now veterans and current service members, understand they can change their ongoing story to a better one.

The final reflection for this material comes from Exodus 18. Jethro, Moses's father-in-law, observed and advised him of what he should do to prevent wearing himself out. When Jethro provided advice, he was serving in the role of a mentor and teacher. This type of influence comes from experience, which reminds us that we do not have to necessarily possess the same skills as the person we are coaching to assist that person in making decisions. Moses made his decisions based on wise counsel, which led Moses to evaluate and appoint chosen leaders. In his role as leader of Israel, Moses guided the people to the farthest point God assigned him to lead. Then, from the process of leader development and appointment, Joshua was chosen to usher God's people into the Promised Land. This is the core of succession planning and coaching: seeing a future that is greater than ourselves.

❚TAKEAWAYS

The servant-leader style has not taken root and developed within some leaders, when compared to other practiced leadership styles in business, but servant leadership has been an operational practice since the beginning of time and a widely faith-based concept and lifestyle, as modeled by Jesus the Christ. Servant leadership begins with a natural desire, first and primarily, to serve others. Servant leaders listen to an individual, value opinions of others, develop trust, develop others, assist others to maneuver through life, encourage, question, display humility, are selfless, and empower others to lead or stand up for what they desire. Servant leaders have both acceptance and empathy, which cause them to accept the person and, if there is a contradiction, to reject performances, behaviors, or beliefs that stagnate forward progress for an individual.

Coaches, mentors, and servant leaders also have been around since the beginning of time; such individuals are vital to facilitating growth in others. The bottom line is this: A coach or organizational leader has the significant opportunity to influence others to make sound, well-grounded decisions to help others in reaching their maximum potential. Coaches and servant leaders empower, encourage, listen, provide empathy, are thinking partners, understand people can rewrite their own story, and are committed to facilitating growth in others. Developmental programs and coaching enhance an individual's decision-making capability. Coaches and servant leaders establish relationships instilled with honesty, vulnerability, and authenticity. Through facilitating the development of a newer awareness, coaches and servant leaders assist others in rewriting their stories.

REFERENCES

Anthony, Erica. L. 2017. "The Impact of Leadership Coaching on Leadership Behaviors." *Journal of Management Development*, 36(7),930–939. https://doi.org/10.1108/JMD-06-2016-0092.

Augustine-Shaw, Donna. 2015. "Leadership and Learning: Identifying an Effective Design For Mentoring New Building Leaders." *Delta Kappa Gamma Bulletin*, 81(2), 21–30.

Autry, James. A. *The Servant Leader: How to Build a Creative Team, Develop Great Morale, and Improve Bottom-Line Performance.* New York: Three Rivers Press, 2004.

Bacharach, Yael. 2013. "5 Essential Skills for Successful Coaching." https://www.inc.com/yael-bacharach/five-essential-skills-for-successful-coaching.html.

Bacon, Terry, R. & Spear, Karen, I. *Adaptive Coaching: The Art and Practice of a Client-Centered Approach to Performance Improvement.* Mountain View: Davis-Black Publishing, 2003.

Bartlett II, James E., Boylan, Robert, V., and Hale, Jimmie, E. 2014. "Executive Coaching: An Integrative Literature Review." *Journal of Human Resource and Sustainability Studies*, 2, 188–195.

Blanchard, Ken. H., Hybels, Bill, and Hodges, Phil. *Leadership By the Book: Tools to Transform Your Workplace.* London: HarperCollins, 2001.

Bloom, Jon. 2017. "Five Marks of a Servant Leader." https://www.desiringgod.org/articles/five-marks-of-a-servant-leader.

Bott, Joyce. (n.d.). "Leadership Styles of Prominent Figures in the Bible." https://www.sophia.org/tutorials/leadership-styles-of-prominent-figures-in-the-bibl.

Brock, Vikki. 2016. "Professional Challenges Facing the Coaching Field from a Historical Perspective." http://libraryofprofessionalcoaching.com/research/history-of-coaching/professional-challenges-facing-the-coaching-field-from-an-historical-perspective.

Burns, James. *Leadership*. New York: HarperCollins Publisher, 1978.

Cameron, Kim S., and Quinn, Robert, E. *Diagnosing and Changing Organizational Culture: Based on Competing Values Framework (3rd ed)*. San Francisco: Jossey-Bass 2011.

Carpenter, Chris. 2014. "Person of Influence: Keys to Being a Great Christian Leader." http://www1.cbn.com/700club/person-influence-keys-being-great-christian-leader.

Collins, Gary. *Christian Coaching: Helping Others Turn Potential Into Reality (2nd ed)*. Colorado Springs: NavPress, 2002.

Collins, Jim. *Good to Great: Why Some Companies Make the Lead … and Others Don't*. New York: HarperCollins, 2001.

Core Competencies. n.d. *ICF*. https://www.coachfederation.org/credential/landing.cfm?ItemNumber=2206.

Duesterhoft, Martha. 2015. 5 "Coaching Skills That Every Manager Needs to Have." https://www.eremedia.com/tlnt/5-coaching-skills-that-every-manager-needs-to-have.

Engstrom, Ted, W. *The Making of a Christian Leader*. Grand Rapids: Pyranee Books, 1976.

Fields, Bea. 2008. "Leadership Coaching: The 360-Degree Review Process." *Fast Company*. https://www.fastcompany.com/939013/leadership-coaching-360-degree-review-process

5 Famous Servant Leaders. n.d. https://futureofworking.com/5-famous-servant-leaders.

Freifeld, Lorri. 2012. "6 Steps to Sustain A Coaching Relationship." *Training: The Source for Professional Development*. https://trainingmag.com/content/6-steps-sustain-coaching-relationship.

Frick, Don, M. (n.d.). "Robert K. Greenleaf Biography." *Greenleaf Center for Servant Leadership*. https://www.greenleaf.org/about-us/robert-k-greenleaf-biography.

Gibson, A. 2012. "Walking in the light." *The Journal of Applied Christian Leadership*, 6(1), 4–8.

Giles, Sunnie. 2016. "The Most Important Leadership Competencies, According to Leaders Around the World." *Harvard Business Review*. https://hbr.org/2016/03/the-most-important-leadership-competencies-according-to-leaders-around-the-world.

Goldsmith, Marshall. *What Got You Here, Won't Get You There: How Successful People Become Even More Successful*. New York: Hachette Book Group, 2007.

Gray, Doug. 2014. "Using Assessments in Leadership Development." *Professional Safety*, 59(7), 23.

Greenleaf, Robert, K. *Servant Leadership: A Journey Into the Nature of Legitimate Power and Greatness (25th ed.)* New York: Paulist Press, 2002.

Greenleaf, Robert K. n.d. Quotes and Sayings. https://www.inspiringquotes.us/author/2597-robert-k-greenleaf.

Harkvay, Daniel. *Becoming a Coaching Leader: The Proven Strategy For Building Your Own Team of Champions*. Nashville: Thomas Nelson, 2007.

Hernez-Broome, Gina, and Hughes, Robert L. 2004. "Leadership Development: Past, Present, and Future." *Human Resource Planning.* http://www.ccl.org/leadership/pdf/research/cclLeadershipDevelopment.pdf.

Hesse, Hermann. *The Journey to The East*. Mansfield Centre: Martino Publishing, 2011.

"Humility." n.d. http://www.christianbiblereference.org/humility.htm.

Hunt, James, M., and Weintraub, Joseph, R. *The Coaching Organization: A Strategy for Developing Leaders*. Thousand Oaks: SAGE, 2007.

Hunter, James, C. *The World's Most Powerful Leadership Principle: How to Become a Servant Leader*. New York: Crown Publishing Group, 2004.

JACL (2012) "Walking in the Light," *Journal of Applied Christian Leadership*: 6 (1), 4-7. https://digitalcommons.andrews.edu/jacl/vol6/iss1/1.

Jennings, Ken, R, and Stahl-Wert, John. *The Serving Leader: Five Powerful Actions to Transform Your Team, Business, and Community*. Oakland: Berrett-Koehler Publisher, 2003.

Kelley, Robert. 1988. "In Praise of Followers." *Harvard Business Review.* https://hbr.org/1988/11/in-praise-of-followers.

Keyser, John. 2014. "What We Can Gain From a 360 Leadership Assessment." https://www.td.org/insights/what-we-can-gain-from-a-360-leadership-assessment.

Kimsey-House, Henry, Kimsey-House, Karen, Sandahl, Phillip, and Whitworth, Laura. *Co-Active Coaching: Changing Business Transforming Lives (3rd ed.)*. Boston: Nicholas Brealey Publishing, 2011.

Kouzes, James, and Posner, Barry. *The Leadership Challenge: How to Make Extraordinary Things Happen in Organizations, (5th. ed.)*. San Francisco: Jossey-Bass, 2012.

Kruse, Kevin. 2015. What Is Leadership? *Forbes*. https://www. forbes.com/sites/kevinkruse/2013/04/09/what-is-leadership/ #18b74815b90c.

Kuhnert, D. *Servant Leadership: Influencing Others to Get There by Leading a Transformational Life*. Bloomington: Author House, 2016.

Levin, Marissa. 2016. "8 Consistent Behaviors of Highly Authentic Leaders." https://www.inc.com/marissa-levin/8-consistent-behaviors-of-highly-authentic-leaders.html.

Lloyd Karina J., Boer, Diana, and Voelpel, Sven C. 2017. "From Listening to Leading: Toward An Understanding of Supervisor Listening Within the Framework of Leader-Member Exchange Theory." *International Journal of Business Communication*, 54(4), 431–451. https://doi.org/10.1177.23.

Malphurs, Aubrey. *Being Leaders: The Nature of Authentic Christian Leadership*. Grand Rapids: Baker Books, 2003.

Markovic, Jovan, McAtavey, Jean, M., and Fischweicher, Priva. 2014. "An Integrative Trust Model in the Coaching Context." *American Journal of Management*, 14(1). 102–110.

Mihiotis, Athanassion and Niki Argirou, N. 2016. "Coaching: From Challenge to Opportunity." *The Journal of Management Development*, 35 (4): 448–463.

Miller, Linda J. and Hall, Chad W. *Coaching for Christian Leaders: A practical guide.* Saint Louis: Chalice Press, 2007.

Naylor, Charles. *Heart Talks.* Oklahoma: Faith Publishing House, 1982.

Northouse, Peter, G. *Leadership: Theory and Practice (6ᵗʰ ed.).* Thousand Oaks: SAGE, 2013.

O'Connor, Joseph and Lages, Allison. 2004. Coaching for Human Development. *International Coaching Community.* http://internationalcoachingcommunity.com/coaching-for-human-development-by-joseph-oconnor-and-andrea-lages.

Palmer, Stephen, and Wybrow, Allison. *The Handbook of Coaching Psychology: A Guide for Practitioners.* New York: Routledge, 2011.

Patterson, Kathleen. 2003. Servant Leadership: A Theoretical Model. *School of Leadership Studies.* https://www.regent.edu/acad/global/publications/sl_proceedings/2003/patterson_servant_leadership.pdf.

Riggio, Ronald. D. 2014. The Top 10 leadership Competencies. *Psychology Today.* https://www.psychologytoday.com/blog/cutting-edge-leadership/201404/the-top-10-leadership-competencies.

Roach, Dale. 2017. 14 Good Quotes About Servant Leaders and More. http://likeateam.com/14-good-quotes-about-servant-leaders-and-more.

Satter, Andrew, and Russ, Diane. 2007. "Why Don't More Senior Leaders Mentor?" *Journal of Management Inquiry,*16 (4), 382-390. doi: 10.1177/105649260730591.

Schein, Edgar. H. *Organizational Culture and Leadership (4ᵗʰ ed).* San Francisco, CA: Jossey-Bass, 2010.

Smith, Ryan. 2014. "5 Ways to Prepare Employees for 360-Degree Feedback." *FastCompany.* https://www.fastcompany.com/3027759/5-ways-to-prepare-your-employees-for-360-degree-feedback.

Spear, Larry. 2010. Character and servant leadership: "Ten Characteristics of Effective, Caring Leaders." *The Journal of Virtues & Leadership, 1(1),* 25-30. https://www.regent.edu/acad/global/publications/jvl/vol1_iss1/Spears_Final.pdf.

Stanley, Andy. *The Next Generation Leader.* Colorado Springs, CO: Multnomah Books, 2003.

Stoltzfus, Tony. *Leadership Coaching: The Disciplines, Skills, and Heart of a Christian Coach.* Virginia Beach, 2005.

Stoltzfus, Tony. 2013. "Practicing Distinctively Christian Life Coaching." http://www.christiancoachingcenter.org/index.php/2013/06/practicing-distinctively-christian-life-coaching-by-tony-stoltzfus.

Stone, A. Gregory, Russell, Robert, F., and Patterson, Kathleen. 2004. "Transformational Versus Servant Leadership: A Difference in Leader Focus." *Leadership & Organization Development Journal, 25(4),* 349-361.

Talley, Henry, C. 2008. Mentoring: The Courage to Cultivate New Leaders. *AANA Journal, 76(5),* 331-4. http://eres.regent.edu.

Ting, Sharon, and Scisco, Peter. *The CCL Handbook of Coaching: A Guide for the Leader Coach.* San Francisco, CA: Jossey-Bass, 2006.

Van Velsor, Ellen, McCauley, Cynthia D., and Ruderman, Marian N. *The Center for Creative Leadership Handbook of Leadership Development* (3rd, ed.) Hoboken: Jossey-Bass, 2010.

Walvoord, John F., and Zuck, Roy, B. *The Bible Knowledge Commentary: An Exposition of the Scriptures.* CO Springs: Victor, 2004.

Webb, Keith E. *Coaching in Ministry: How Busy Church Leaders Can Multiply Their Ministry Impact.* Bellevue: Active Results LLC, 2015.

"What Is Christian Life Coaching?" n.d. http://christianlifecoaching. com/christian-life-coaching.

Whitmore, John. *Coaching for Performance: GROWing Human Potential and Purpose (4th ed.).* Boston: Hatchett Book Group, 2009.

Wildflower, Leni, and Brennan, Diane. *The Handbook of Knowledge-Based Coaching.* San Francisco: Jossey-Bass, 2011.

Wimer, Scott., and Nowack, Kenneth, M. 2006. "13 Common Mistakes Using 360 Degree Feedback." http://www. retroalimentame.com.mx/informacion/downloads/13%20 Common%20Mistakes.pdf.

Wright, N.T. *After You Believe: Why Christian Character Matters.* New York: HarperCollins, 2010.

Zenger, Jack. 2016. "How Effective Are Your 360-Degree Feedback Assessments?" *Forbes.com.* https://www.forbes.com/ sites/jackzenger/2016/03/10/how-effective-are-your-360-degree-feedback-assessments/#67ded6e2a690.

Printed in the United States
By Bookmasters